The Sangh & Swaraj

Role of RSS in Freedom Struggle

When we write history of Indian independence struggle, we cannot forget the role played by tribal leaders like Birsa Munda of Madhya Bharat, Rani Gaidinliu in North East and Alluri Sitarama Raju in Southern Bharat. This book reaffirms that a swayamsevak will pay any price, bear any burden, meet any hardship, support any friend, oppose any foe to protect and preserve Bharat.

—Ravi Kumar

Scholar, Writer, Senior Prachaarak of RSS

❖❖❖

Sangh swayamsevaks were taught by the founder of RSS, Dr. Hedgewar, to plunge into national work with no expectation of recognition, just as one serves one's mother. It was therefore natural that documentation of their contributions to the motherland was not a priority. In that background, this book is a commendable effort to bring to the fore, the contribution of the Sangh swayamsevaks in restoration of true Swaraj for all.

—Ayush Nadimpalli

Writer & Gen. Secretary Samvit Kendra, Hyderabad

❖❖❖

This book, through information and insights, brings out contribution of RSS leaders during India's freedom movement and the organisation's service in helping displaced Hindu/Sikh refugees in the states of Punjab & Jammu-Kashmir, not to forget relief camps in Bengal & Assam. It also delves on Guruji Golwalkar's meetings with the Maharaja of J&K before Hari Singh signed the Instrument of Accession for State's merger with India'.

—Sanjeev Nayyar

Founder, www.esamskriti.com, Independent Researcher

The Sangh & Swaraj

Role of RSS in Freedom Struggle

Ratan Sharda

PRABHAT
PRAKASHAN

Published by
PRABHAT PRAKASHAN PVT. LTD.
4/19 Asaf Ali Road,
New Delhi-110 002 (INDIA)
e-mail: prabhatbooks@gmail.com

ISBN 978-93-5322-241-3
THE SANGH & SWARAJ
by Shri Ratan Sharda

Edition
2026

Paperback Price
₹ 200.00 (Rupees Two Hundred only)

Printed at
Narula Printers, Delhi

I dedicate this book to thousands of unnamed, unsung swayamsevaks who sacrificed their lives, families and homes to save Hindu and Sikh brethren. And, to millions of our own for whom Independence day brought untold misery and pain before they could breath free.

"Liberating our intellect from the values (sanskaars) of other countries and evolving a system (tantra) of growth with our own feelings and will is 'swa-tantra' (system by self). But, a system that is born through ignoring our history, being slaves of intellect of others, inspired by other societies will not be 'swa-tantra' but 'para-tantra' (system of others, or slavery of others). A system based on Russia's directions will be a 'Russian-tantra', not 'swa-tantra'. A system inspired by the politicians of England, under their guardianship or their support, will be England's system. A federal system created with inspiration of free America would be an American system, never 'swa-tantra'."

–Shri Guruji in 1947

Guruji Samagra, Page 169-170

Preface

Various publications from earlier times till recently have information about work done by Rashtriya Swayamsevak Sangh (RSS) in pre-independence era of India and the role it played in independence struggle of India. However, of late, political compulsions have made Left and so-called secular parties run malicious propaganda about its role in independence struggle and its sterling record of public service in every field including wars, to create doubts in the mind of the people. There is a consensus that the Congress party of that time was an umbrella organisation for all political shades for a common cause – that is to attain freedom. There were leaders who led other organisations and political groups also even as they remained leaders of Congress.

Three major non-violent movements for freedom were launched under Gandhiji's leadership in 1921, 1930 and 1942. There is no doubt that Gandhiji's biggest contribution was to involve common men and women in the freedom struggle in a simple and easily understandable form. Millions got involved in this struggle because of his innovative approach.

RSS founder Dr. K.B. Hedgewar took part in each of these movements when he was a Congress leader and even later after he had founded the RSS. He died in 1940. A large number of RSS swayamsevaks and leaders took an active part in 1942 Quit India movement too. They participated as common citizens, as per the guidelines laid down by Dr. Hedgewar. Another important aspect of the Indian independence struggle that was fought over a long period was the armed revolt by many patriots. Beginning from 1857, followed by Chaphekar brothers, Birsa Munda, Rani Gaidinliu, Alluri Sitarama Raju, Savarkar, Chandrashekhar Azad, Bhagat Singh, Madanlal Dhingra, Rashbehari Bose to Subhash Chandra Bose and his Indian National Army (INA), we have a virtual roll of honour of hundreds of such dare devil freedom fighters. However, a narrative being set since 1947 and more vigorously now, is that it was the non-violent movement or one party that brought independence to India. This is a simplistic view of current history, if not deliberate. It is like saying that 100th blow of a hammer broke a rock and earlier 99 blows had no role.

My last book 'RSS3600 – Demystifying Rashtriya Swayamsevak Sangh' – has annexures that contain information about RSS participation in independence struggle, background of the ban on RSS and subsequent unconditional lifting of ban. The only condition imposed was to submit a written Constitution. It was an ironical face saving excuse since Congress itself did not have a written Constitution for 15 years after its foundation. Various references to this period established that the ban was more out of jealousy for a highly popular organisation. This fear of the rise of a popular political alternative was a sign of irrational thinking because Shri Madhav Sadashiv Golwalkar, aka Shri Guruji, the second RSS Sarsanghchaalak, had time and again reiterated that RSS had no interest in becoming a political party.

Persecution of RSS by the Congress party had begun months before Gandhiji's assassination at the peak of relief work being done by RSS for the unfortunate citizens of Bharat who were supported very poorly by the government in the wake of the Partition.

After reading these annexures in RSS 3600 based mostly on the highly researched biography of Shri Guruji written by an RSS veteran thinker Shri Ranga Hari. Some friends felt that I should expand this theme and highlight RSS's role in freedom struggle as a separate document. This is how the idea of this book took root.

I have tried to keep this monograph short and picked up only those facts and those stories that are well referenced. Ideally, oral records and testimonials collected in such turbulent times are considered valid and reliable records in history writing. There are personal witness accounts picked up from some well documented books. There was no system of audio or video recording at that time for common people. There are hundreds of personal oral experiences that old RSS workers share, some writings are scattered in small booklets and individual memoirs of RSS workers in different languages across India who had lived through those disturbing times. As a mark of respect to unknown martyrs of that time, I could have compiled a massive volume by quoting all the material available. But, the idea was to create an easily referenceable document. This book gives us an idea that RSS was wedded to the cause of Swaraj or Independence since inception and was preparing for a long drawn battle for which it was preparing its cadre. British records stand testimony to this resolve.

As a prologue, I have taken liberty to publish a set of scanned images of a handwritten list of RSS swayamsevaks and other well-known Hindu and Sikh brethren of Amritsar who were killed while defending their brethren. I had chanced upon this old document in RSS documentation centre in Delhi while researching for my thesis on RSS resolutions. You suddenly confront the past ghosts when you see this meticulously prepared list.

RSS cadre had not been too keen about proper documentation since the beginning. However, lot of attention is being paid now to this important aspect. Reason for this lack of documentation could be that Dr. Hedgewar and his successor Shri Guruji were strictly averse to publicising RSS work or projecting themselves. They said, "We should be *prasiddhi paraangmukh*", that is, keep away from publicity; and work silently for the society and motherland. This small contribution tries to cover this lacuna in RSS literature to some extent. I hope that this small book will be useful to the people who genuinely wish to know about this critical part of RSS history.

I humbly thank Shri Manmohan Vaidya for sparking the the idea of this book in my mind and Shri Milnd Oak, CEO of Bharati Web for cross checking all my references painstakingly.

—Ratan Sharda

25th December, 2018

Contents

RSS swayamsevaks and other well known citizens killed in Amritsar in 1946-47

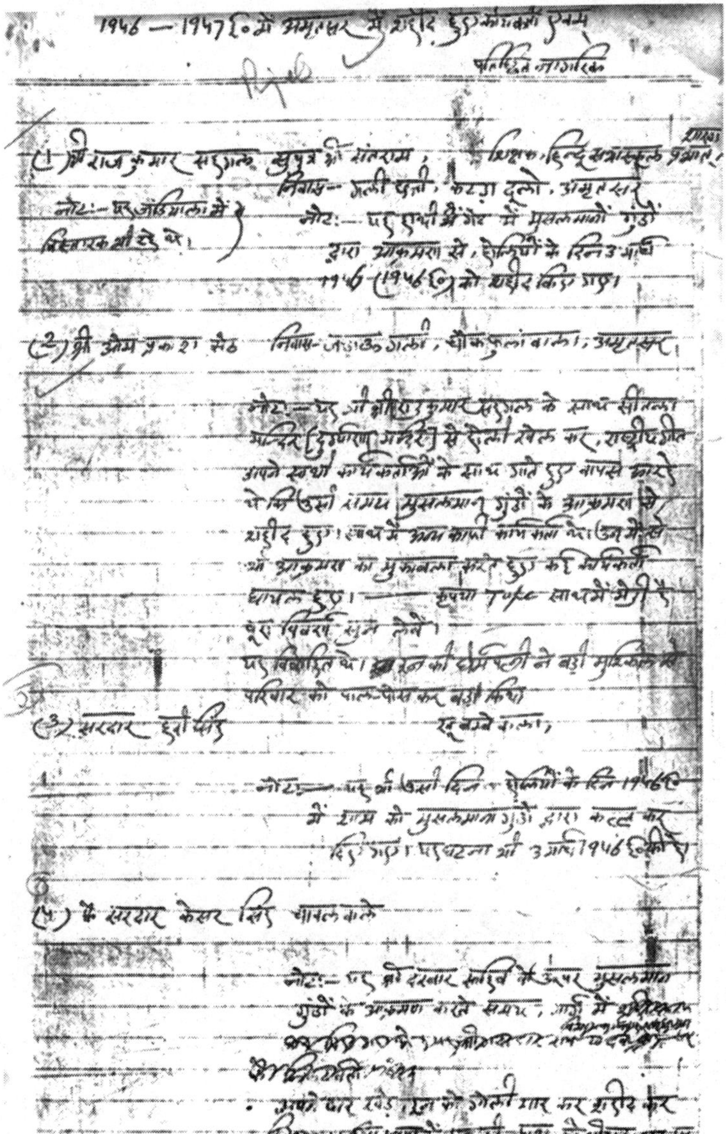

1946 — 1947 ई० में अमृतसर में शहीद हुए कार्यकर्ता एवम् प्रतिष्ठित नागरिक

(1) श्री राज कुमार सहगल, सुपुत्र श्री संतराम, शिक्षक, हिन्दू सभा स्कूल [illegible]
निवास— गली पत्ती, कटड़ा दूलो, अमृतसर
नोट:— यह [illegible] गेट में मुसलमानों गुंडों द्वारा आक्रमण से, होलियों के दिन 3 मार्च 1946 (1946 ई०) को शहीद किए गए।

नोट:— यह जंडियाला में विस्तारक भी रहे थे।

(2) श्री ओम प्रकाश सेठ निवास— जंडाऊ गली, चौक फुलांवाला, अमृतसर।

नोट:— यह श्री राज कुमार सहगल के साथ सीतला मन्दिर (दुर्गियाना मन्दिर) से होली खेल कर, राष्ट्रीय गीत अपने साथी कार्यकर्ताओं के साथ गाते हुए वापस आ रहे थे कि उसी समय मुसलमान गुंडों के आक्रमण से शहीद हुए। साथ में अन्य काफी कार्यकर्ता थे। उन में से भी आक्रमण का मुकाबला करते हुए कई कार्यकर्ता घायल हुए। —— कृपया Tape साथ में भेजी है पूरे विवरण सुन लेवें।
यह विवाहित थे। इन की धर्मपत्नी ने बड़ी मुश्किल से परिवार को पाल-पोस कर बड़ा किया

(3) सरदार हरी सिंह [illegible] वाला,

नोट:— यह भी उसी दिन होलियों के दिन 1946 ई० में शाम को मुसलमान गुंडों द्वारा कत्ल कर दिए गए। यह घटना भी 3 मार्च 1946 ई० की है।

(4) सरदार केसर सिंह [illegible] वाले

नोट:— यह श्री दरबार साहिब के ऊपर मुसलमान गुंडों के आक्रमण करते समय, [illegible] में [illegible]
[illegible]
अपने घर खड़े, इन को गोली मार कर शहीद कर दिया गया। [illegible] इन की लाश को [illegible]

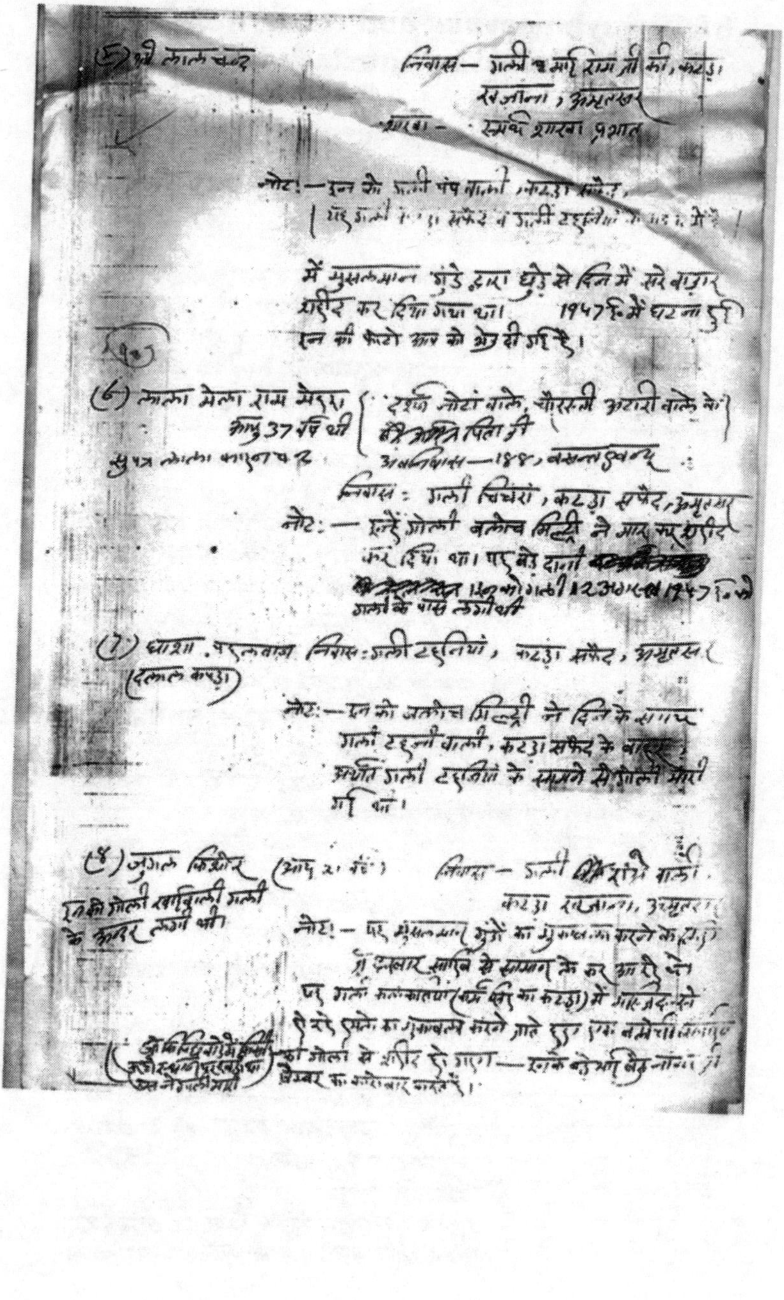

(5) श्री लाल चन्द — निवास — गली [illegible] राम जी की, कटड़ा खज़ाना, अमृतसर

शाखा — [illegible] शाखा प्रभात

नोट! — इन को गली [illegible] वाली, कटड़ा सफैद, [illegible] गली [illegible] सफैद व गली टहलियां [illegible]

में मुसलमान गुंडे द्वारा छुरे से दिन में सरे बाज़ार शहीद कर दिया गया था। 1947 ई० में घटना हुई इन की फोटो आप को भेज दी गई है।

(6) लाला मेला राम मेहरा, आयु 37 वर्ष थी, सुपुत्र लाला [illegible]

[दर्शन [illegible] वाले, चौरस्ती अटारी वाले के [illegible] पिता जी — अब निवास — 188, बसन्त [illegible]]

निवास : गली चिचरां, कटड़ा सफैद, अमृतसर

नोट: — इन्हें गोली बलोच मिल्ट्री ने मार कर शहीद कर दिया था। यह बड़े दानी ~~[illegible]~~ [illegible] गोली 12 अगस्त 1947 ई० को गली के पास लगी थी

(7) धारा [illegible] निवास : गली टहलियां, कटड़ा सफैद, अमृतसर (दलाल कटड़ा)

नोट: — इन को बलोच मिल्ट्री ने दिन के समय गली टहलीं वाली, कटड़ा सफैद के बाहर, अर्थात गली टहलियां के सामने से गोली मारी गई थी।

(8) जुगल किशोर (आयु 21 वर्ष) — निवास — गली [illegible] वाली, कटड़ा खज़ाना, अमृतसर

इनको गोली [illegible] गली के अन्दर लगी थी

नोट! — यह मुसलमान गुंडों का मुकाबला करने के [illegible] [illegible] बाज़ार [illegible] से सामान ले कर आ रहे थे जब गली [illegible] (कटड़ा) में [illegible] हो रहे हमले का मुकाबला करने गये हुए एक [illegible] की गोली से शहीद हो गए — इनके [illegible] [illegible] का [illegible] करते हैं।

([illegible] ने गोली मारी)

1947 ई० में शहीद कार्यकर्ता

(9) श्री लाल चन्द खन्ना — निवास – गली बद्रीनाथ, कटड़ा परजा, अमृतसर

(10) श्री पन्ना लाल — निवास – गली बद्रीनाथ, कटड़ा परजा, अमृतसर

(11) श्री नन्द लाल मेहता, गली नैन सुख, कटड़ा परजा, अमृतसर

नोट :– इन को लेकर मस्जिद से मुसलमानो द्वारा अपने घर के ऊपर खड़े गोली लगी थी। घटना सन् 1947 ई० में हुई।

नोट : इन का फोटो आप को भेजा जा रहा है

(12) सरदारी लाल — गली नैन सुख, कटड़ा परजा,

नोट :– इन को भी अपने घर के ऊपर गोली लगी थी। गोली मुसलमानों ने मारी थी।

(13) श्री गोपाल दास — निवास :– गली तेलियां, नमक मंडी,

1947 ई० की घटना :— अपने घर पर बम बनाते हुए इन के हाथ में बम फट गया। जिस से इन की [illegible] मृत्यु हो गई। उस समय रात के 11 बजे थे और कर्फ्यू लगा हुआ था।

(उस समय कोठे पर 9 (नौ) कार्यकर्ता थे। वे सब घायल हो गए थे। उन में अधिक घायल होने वालों में श्री गोपाल जौहरी, तिलक राज जौहरी, व श्री मनोहर लाल जी [प्रचलित शस्त्रों के मुख्य अधिकारी, कटड़ा आहलूवालिया वाले] थे। ये सब लगभग तीन मास बाद, चलने फिरने लग गए थे।

(14) गोटी पहलवान

दुकानदार, चौक लछमनसर में चांदी के बरतन बनाते थे।
नोट = 1947 ई० में अकालियों वाला बाजार के निकट इन के हाथ में बम फट गया था जिस से इन की उसी समय मृत्यु हो गई। इन का शरीर बड़ा गठीला था। इन जैसी हस्ती शायद ही किसी की होगी।
मृत्यु समय इन की आयु 30 वर्ष थी।
यह मुसलमान गुंडों की गोली-बारी का मुकाबला (प्रतिरोध) करने जाते हुए मर गए।
कुछ लोग यह भी बताते हैं कि यह उस समय शराब के नशे में थे। — तब इन की आयु 30 वर्ष थी

(15) - - - - - एक गुमनाम शहीद

नोट। — इन का नाम मालूम नहीं हो सका
यह सेवा सोसाइटी, फायर ब्रिगेड, हाल बाजार में कर्मचारी थे। — लेडा बाज़ार, कटड़ा करम सिंह में मुसलमानों द्वारा हिन्दुओं के मकानों में लगाई आग को बुझाते हुए गोली लगने से शहीद हो गए

नोट:— यह वर्णन श्री अमर नाथ शर्मा (आजाद) नमक मंडी वालों ने करवाया। यह सन 1947 ई० में सेवा सोसाइटी फायर-ब्रिगेड, हाल बाजार, अमृतसर के मुख्य अधिकारी थे।

(16) सतपाल

कटड़ा करम सिंह, निकट गली लाहौरियां पर मुसलमानों द्वारा शहीद कर दिए गए थे। — यह वर्णन श्री जागीरी लाल (पुष्पराज) ने लिखवाया
नोट। — जागीरी लाल जी गली लाहौरियां वाले द्वारा 1947 ई० का विस्तार से वर्णन Tape द्वारा किया गया था। आप Tape सुन लेवें। Tape आप को भेज दी गई है।

(17) जगदीश "श्री भाटिया" निवास = गली सतोवाली, निमकमंडी
S/o [illegible] [illegible] कटड़ा करम सिंह, साथम हलवा
बंदीकले
घटना — [illegible] अपने 10–12 [illegible] के साथ, [illegible] से बन्द [illegible] में [illegible] मिल्ट्री द्वारा [illegible]।

नोट — आज भी गली सतोवाली के मुख्य द्वार पर "श्री जगदीश भाटिया गेट" नाम खुदा है। [illegible] इन की यह वीरता-पूर्ण [illegible] अमृतसर में प्रसिद्ध है। इनकी दोनों बहनें दिल्ली में रहती हैं — फोटो नहीं मिल सकी —

(18) "श्री सुदर्शन भाटिया" निवास — गली संगोवाली, नमकमंडी, S/o श्री मास्टर किशनचन्द भाटिया — साथम हलवा।

1947 ई० जब [illegible] गली [illegible] को पार करते समय सामने से मियाँ नाम के मुसलमान द्वारा चलाई गोली इन की गर्दन के आर पार हो गई। और यह वीर वहीं ढेर हो गए।
मरने से कुछ दिन पूर्व बम बनाते समय [illegible] जैसी कोई चीज़ पड़ गई थी। तब से इन की आंखों में धुंधला-पन रहने लगा था परन्तु यह (उस [illegible] की [illegible] नहीं) करते थे। — यह जगदीश भाटिया (शहीद) के रिश्तेदार थे।

(19) किरपाराम निवास — कुल्ली घर, अमृतसर

नोट: — यह [illegible] [illegible] हमले के समय वीरता पूर्वक शहीद हो गए थे।
इस घटना का पूर्ण [illegible] श्री [illegible] [illegible], गली संगोवाली, अमृतसर ने लिखवाया है। [illegible] यह विवरण [illegible] से [illegible] कर भेजा गया है। कृपया पढ़ लेवें। — इस [illegible] में अमृतसर के भी [illegible] [illegible] 17–18

(20) राम लुभाया सेठ (23 वर्ष आयु) निवास — गली कलालां, खू सुनियारियां, सुपुत्र श्री देवी दास — अंधा खरसां।
नोट: — इन को कटड़ा [illegible] में [illegible] हिन्दुओं की रक्षा करते हुए बलोच मिल्ट्री की गोली लगी।
(उस वक्त गली वाले श्री रोशन लाल सेठ इन को उठा कर हस्पताल ले

लेकिन जहां इन की मृत्यु हो गई। यह विवाहित थे और इनके तीन बच्चे थे। जो कि अब भी इनके पुराने [illegible] पर रह रहे हैं। इनके बड़े पुत्र श्री [illegible] [illegible] हैं। [illegible] [illegible] धर्मपत्नी ने शुरू 2 में अपने बच्चों को बड़ी कठिनाई से पाला-पोसा। भगवान की कृपा से आजकल (1997 ई० में) इन की आर्थिक स्थिति काफी अच्छी है।

21) लाला ठाकुर दास खन्ना   दुकान :– लाला खज़ाना मल बंजवारीलाल, बाज़ार घंटा घर, अमृतसर

सुपुत्र, लाला खज़ाना मल
निवास = कटड़ा भाई संत सिंह
मृत्यु :– [illegible] 7 [illegible] 1947 ई०

यह [illegible] [illegible] के थे। इन्हें कटड़ा भाई संत सिंह चौक के पास बाज़ार [illegible] की नुक्कड़ (दुकान के [illegible] के पास) पर [illegible] छुरा मारकर शहीद कर दिया गया। छुरा मारने वाला उस गली का नामी बदमाश था। उस मुसलिम गुंडे का नाम कुब्बा कसाई था। कई लोग इसे कुब्बा पहलवान भी कहते थे।

इस कत्ल के बाद कुछ दिनों बाद जब लाला ठाकुर दास का लड़का जुगल किशोर यह समाचार सुन कर बाहर से आया तो उस ने [illegible] से राइफल ले कर कई मुसलिम गुंडों को मार कर बदला चुकाया। वैसे भी यह N.C.C. के Camp से उस समय वापस आया था। शस्त्र चलाने का अभ्यास उसे पहले से ही था।

नोट :– यह [illegible] [illegible] [illegible] [illegible] [illegible] [illegible] [illegible] [illegible] [illegible] [illegible] [illegible] [illegible] [illegible] [illegible]

22) पंडित मुनीलाल   निवास – [illegible] [illegible], कटड़ा [illegible]

घटना :– इन के पांव में बलोच-पुलिस ने गोली मारी थी। बाद में 2 दिनों बाद हस्पताल में इन की मृत्यु हो गई थी।

नोट :– ये [illegible] [illegible] [illegible] [illegible] [illegible] [illegible] [illegible] [illegible] [illegible] [illegible] [illegible] इनको आंखों देखा बताया है।

1947 ई० में शहीद अमृतसर

(23) कृष्णा लाल) गली कर्मों वाली, करमों ड्योढ़ी, अमृतसर
घटना — घर पर बम फटने से मृत्यु 1947 ई०
घर की छत भी उड़ गई थी।

(24) श्यामलाल रंगवाले
घटना — कटड़ा [illegible] में कत्ल हुए।
इसके बाद मुस्लिम गुंडों पर हमला किया गया,
चौक [illegible] में मुस्लिम लोगों गुंडे का कत्ल हुआ
जिस में रक्षा लाला, गली [illegible] वाले का
नाम [illegible] गया था।

(25-26) सरदार हरीसिंह व अमर सिंह (दोनों पिता-पुत्र)
चौक पशमवाला (चौक फरीद) अमृतसर
इन दोनों को मुसलमानों ने चौक फरीद में
निकट, गली घजूरियां में कत्ल कर दिया था।

(27) राम लोक शर्मा (आयु 45 वर्ष थी) (चपरासी [illegible] स्कूल,) पी. पी. ब्रांच,
इस को बाज़ार चमड़े वाला, निकट मन्दिर भैरों में छुरी मार कर
शहीद कर दिया गया था।

28) पुजारी पंडित बंसीलाल का पुत्र'' यह ठाकुर द्वारा शंकर दास की कहलाता है
यहां पर पुजारी और पुत्र रहते थे। यहां मन्दिर में पुत्र
को मुसलमानों ने गोली मार कर शहीद कर दिया था।
पुत्र मन्दिर में ही मर गया था। — कर्फ्यू लगा होने
के कारण उस का संस्कार भी मन्दिर में करना पड़ा था।

29) चौकीदार (पहरेदार) इसको गली घजूरियां, बाज़ार चमड़े वाले में
पहरेदारी करते समय, बलोची सिपाही ने गोली मार
कर शहीद कर दिया।

Chapter–1

Dr. Hedgewar – A Patriot and a Freedom Fighter

"Just as it is true that one should always be ready to be imprisoned, or be sent to Kalapani, or get hanged; it is equally true that one should not at all be in confusion that going to prison is like reaching heavens; as if this imprisonment itself means achieving freedom. One should definitely not understand that filling prisons will get us freedom or swaraajya. The truth is that one can serve the nation in many ways by being out of prison."

–Dr. K.B. Hedgewar, addressing people after receiving 1 year imprisonment order in 1921

(N.H. Palkar, Dr. Hedgewar, page 91)

Dr. Hedgewar was a strong-willed person, who had lost his parents to the outbreak of cholera very early in his life, thus leading a life of penury, but never missing sight of the objective of his life – that was to free Mother India. Many stories of his activities as head-strong patriotic young child abound, telling us about his intense fervour at an age when children just wish to play games. However, his agitation while he was in Matric (SSC of today) in Neil City School is noteworthy. As a protest against infamous 'Risley Circular', that had banned the slogan of '*Vande Maataram*' in 1906, he organised students of his school secretively to raise the slogan of '*Vande Maataram*' when the school inspector came to visit the school. When the inspector threatened action, the agitation intensified with boycotting the class. This went on for nearly a month. No student would divulge his name inspite of threats of dismissal. Ultimately, he himself came into open as he didn't want his friends to suffer. He was dismissed from that school.[1]

His tryst with revolutionaries in Kolkata where he went to study medicine and became a doctor is documented by his biographers. His compatriot in Anusheelan Samiti, Shri Trailokyanath Chakravarty, mentions him and his work in his autobiography, '*Jail Mein Tees Baras*'. He also published his photograph as a team member in this book.[2] His code name in the police files was 'cocain'.[3] His colleagues used to recount his absence from guest house at odd hours in the night.

After he finished his doctor's degree, he returned to Nagpur to pursue his dream of freeing India. He refused to marry as he had decided to dedicate his life for the national cause. He had seen that most of the leaders of freedom struggle were married. He believed that this could distract him from doing his duty.[5] He had realised by that time that sporadic violent acts won't be able to dislodge the British and chose the path of non-violent struggle and joined Congress.

Dr. K.B. Hedgewar – a committed Congress party member

Dr. Hedgewar was joint organiser of the national session of the Indian National Congress in 1920 in Nagpur along with Dr. Hardikar. They recruited about 1,200 volunteers for the purpose. Dr. Hedgewar was the joint secretary of Nagpur branch of the Indian National Congress at that time. He did such a wonderful job that his stature in the party and his following rose sharply. Congress till that time was only demanding 'Self-rule' as a dominion under British rule. It followed the same line in that session too. However, Dr. Hedgewar had presented a resolution to the resolution committee, of which he was a member that demanded 'Complete Freedom'. It was rejected by the committee.

The proposed resolution said – "*Goal of Congress is to achieve complete freedom and establishing Indian republic and to liberate other nations of the world from exploitation and atrocities of capitalist imperialism*."[6] Periodical Modern Review wrote in March 1921 issue, "But the proposed resolution, which excited laughter among serious-minded people, deserved a better fate than what it met with the subject committee.[7] This session would also be remembered for long for untimely death of Lokmanya Tilak just before the session. He was to preside over the session. This session saw the beginning of the rise of Gandhiji as the unrivalled Congress leader.

It is noteworthy that Congress declared its resolve for complete independence only after 9 years in 1929 Lahore Conference. It shows that Dr. Hedgewar was much ahead of the leaders of his times about his vision for India – not just to be an independent country, but also help other colonized countries to gain independence from what he termed 'Capitalist Imperialism'.

First Imprisonment

His first imprisonment was for taking part in '*Non-Cooperation movement*' in 1921. This movement took place around the same time that *Khilaafat* agitation gathered momentum with active support of Gandhiji and Congress. There was disquiet in Congress about support to Khilaafat agitation, especially in Nagpur that was a major centre of followers of Lokmanya Tilak. They felt that linking Khilaafat to freedom movement was not a good idea.

Though Dr. Hedgewar too was against Khilaafat agitation, he did not want Gandhiji's 'non-Cooperation movement' to be weakened. Therefore, he jumped into Non-cooperation movement with full energy so that the larger fight for freedom from colonial rule did not suffer. To give Non-Cooperation movement a push, Dr. Chaulkar, Samimullah Khan and Dr. Hedgewar became very active.[8] It shows his sagacity and commitment to freedom movement that Doctorji worked even with avid supporter of Khilaafat agitation, Samimullah Khan for the sake of providing momentum to the Non-Cooperation movement.

Dr. Hedgewar gave highly aggressive speeches with Dr. Munje for 2-3 months in many places like Bhandara, Khapa, Kelwad, Talegaon, Dashasahasra, Deoli, Vardha, Bori, etc. To stop him, the district collector Cyril James Irwin banned his public speaking and holding meetings for one year, vide a notice dated 23 February, 1921.[8A] He did not stop his meetings. Finally, he was put on trial in May 1921 for his 'objectionable speeches'. His defence on 5th August was so fiery that the judge Smelly exclaimed, "*His statement of defence is more seditious than his speech*!"[9] He was given one year imprisonment on 19th August.[10] Excerpt of his inspiring speech while going to the jail is quoted at the beginning of this chapter –

"Just as it is true that one should always be ready to be imprisoned, or be sent to Kalapani, or get hanged, it is equally true that one should not at all be in confusion that going to prison is like reaching heavens, as if this imprisonment itself means achieving freedom. One should definitely not understand that filling prisons will get us freedom or swaraajya. The truth

is that one can serve the nation in many ways by being out of prison."

When he came out of prison on 12 July, 1922, he was given a rousing welcome despite a heavy downpour. He was given a huge public reception in the evening in Venkatesh Theatre due to inclement weather. Top national leaders of Congress came to fete him. They included Hakim Ajmal Khan, Pandit Motilal Nehru, Rajagopalachari, Dr. Ansari, Vitthalbhai Patel, and Kasturirangan Iyengar. Pandit Motilal Nehru and Hakim Ajmal Khan too spoke in this programme. In his speech in front of the multitude, Dr. Hedgewar said, *"Just being a state guest in a prison for one year does not mean that my qualification has increased, nor has it given me a new identity for the world. If at all, my qualification does seem to have increased, one must thank the government for this.... It will not be ideal to have any goal less than full freedom."*[11] We find a sense of self-abnegation that was the hallmark of all his acts throughout his life and so also of RSS, viz. keeping social interest above self-interest and keeping away from self-promotion.

Key is Unity and Self-Sacrifice

After his release, he kept working for Congress at various levels. He was elected as the joint Secretary of the State Congress Committee in 1922. There was a tendency at that time too to take extreme positions. There used to be avoidable verbal clashes to defeat others' ideas. In 1921, there was a move to pass a resolution criticising the revolutionaries under the Chairmanship of Loknayak Aney in Madhya Prant. Dr. Hedgewar reasoned with the committee that even if the committee did not wish to follow the path of revolutionaries, its members should not doubt their patriotism.[12] He kept away from various group formations like Tilak-Gandhi,

Violence-Non-violence, and Congress-Revolutionaries, etc. To him attaining freedom was more important than these binaries, personalities and specific path. Pandit Ramgopal Vidyalankar recalled, "Doctor would keep affectionate relations even if there was difference of opinion. Therefore, whenever I went to his home, he would laugh heartily and tell me, I welcome you but not your views."[13] Similarly, he had excellent relations with Advocate Ruikar who was a committed Communist.

Mahatma Gandhi was sentenced to 6 years of imprisonment on 18th March, 1922. It was decided to have a Gandhi Day on the every 18th of month till he was released. On this date in October, we hear Dr. Hedgewar on Gandhiji thus, "The day today is very pious. This is the day to hear and ponder over the great qualities of a great man like Gandhiji . … *The greatest quality of Gandhiji is readiness for self-sacrifice for the work taken up till it reaches its conclusion*. This is the most important quality that disciples of his movement need to learn – self-sacrifice and to give up selfishness. Second is to avoid duplicity in speech and action."[14]

Allergy to any kind of discipline in the name of non-violence within Congress is highlighted in an interesting episode during this time. Dr. N.S. Hardikar formed Hindusthani Seva Dal in 1923 during the Congress session in Kakinada to create a sense of discipline in Congress volunteers. However, there was strong criticism from Congress leaders. Pandit Nehru was surprised at this strong reaction though Seva Dal had many luminous Congress leaders. He wrote, "*We were surprised to find later how much opposition there was to the Seva Dal among the leading Congressmen*. Some said that this was a dangerous departure, as it meant introducing military element in the Congress and the military arm might overpower the civil authority! Others seemed to think that the only discipline necessary was for the volunteer to obey orders issued from above and for the rest it was hardly desirable for volunteers even to walk in step. At the back of the mind of some was the notion that *the idea of having trained and drilled volunteers was somewhat inconsistent with the Congress' principle of non-violence*."[15] Doctor Hedgewar was against the view that you needed 'yes sir' kind of volunteers only for laying *durries* and chairs. This strange obsession of dominant section of Congress with non-discipline could be the reason behind the anarchic way our republic and its politics have evolved.

Dr. Hedgewar's Decision to Reform Hindu Society

While being active in freedom movement, one question always bothered Dr. Hedgewar. How could a handful of British coming from 7,000 km across the seas rule over our huge nation? He realised that there was something wrong with us. In his years in public life, he realised that our society had forgotten its own history and was fragmented on lines of caste, language and regionalism. He saw that it was disorganised and stifled by oppressive customs that could be exploited by the British. If we did not change even after gaining independence, history could repeat itself. Tweedledum would replace Twidlidee, that's all. Therefore, *the most important fundamental work seemed to raise the nation above caste and creed, reform it, organise it, help get it rid of its oppressive customs, raise its national consciousness. He could see that it was possible only by keeping away from politics, propaganda and working silently in a sustained manner.*[16]

With this thought in mind, he founded Rashtriya Swayamsevak Sangh in 1925 on Vijayadashami day in a meeting with 22 colleagues of his, at his home. The new organisation's name 'Rashtriya Swayamsevak Sangh' was decided in April 1926 by the team that had announced its formation some months back, not by Dr. Hedgewar. Here, we see another characteristic of RSS, that is caring more for the work than the paper work or urge to get a label or name first. The methodology of daily gathering, called shakhas, was an innovative idea. Even after establishing RSS, he had warm relations with political and social leaders of all shades and opinions.

This organisation, *RSS, was born not due to political differences with any leader or political party but with a clear positive thought and idea of organising and reforming Hindu society*. It was not a decision born out of negativity against any person or community.

Dr. Hedgewar could have stayed back in Congress and become a prominent leader. But, he chose a different path, a more difficult path where he pushed himself beyond very limit of human endurance and dedication to bring up a new organisation based on sacrifice, selfless service and strong sense of brotherly affection. As a fledgling organisation that worked for creating disciplined patriot citizens with character, it was a long haul for RSS. Moulding human beings is a slow process. But, by 1930, RSS had spread its wings a little in the neighbouring regions of Nagpur.

Total Commitment to Complete Freedom

In the Lahore session of All India Congress Committee in December 1929, Congress declared 'Complete Independence' as its goal. In line with this goal, a resolution was passed to celebrate 26th January, 1930 as Independence Day. Dr. Hedgewar sent out a notification to all his RSS shakhas – "We all are very happy to see that AICC has spelt out its goal very clearly. So, it is our duty to support and cooperate with this organisation. It is but natural. As a part of this duty, all shakhas should come together on the evening of 26th January, 1930 at 6 p.m.; salute the national flag, i.e. *bhagwa* flag. At this time, the meaning of freedom and the objective of that flow from these words should be explained to people collected there. *And Congress has taken this up as its goal. Therefore, we should complement Congress*. Information about these programmes should be sent to us."[17] (According to a paper of India Policy Foundation and a website specialising in flags, crwflags.com, recommendation of the flag committee of AICC till that time was rectangular *bhagwa* flag with a *charkha* in left corner.[18])

Fighting for Freedom as a Citizen under Congress Umbrella

A new agitation – Non-cooperation Movement (*Savinay Avagyaa Andolan*) was launched in 1930 by Mahatma Gandhi in the form of 'Daandi March' or Salt satyagraha. The agitation began in Akola on 2nd April, 1930. In Madhya prant, it was decided by Congress to add Jungle satyagraha to this Salt satyagraha since there were no salt pans there and British had put in a law to curtail people's rights over jungles.[19]

Many swayamsevaks had begun taking part in this agitation from its very inception. In November 1929, senior RSS workers had a 3-day-long meeting to decide what should be RSS's role in this agitation. It was decided that RSS would give unconditional support to it. By 1929, there were Sangh shakhas in 37 villages in Vidarbha. In Wardha, there were 12 shakhas. By 1930, this number had risen to 30. Once Dr. Hedgewar decided to take part in it, there was a huge backing to it from all around.[20]

On 12th July, the Guru Purnima festival day in RSS shakha, Dr. Hedgewar shared his decision to participate in the satyagraha and resigned as the Sarsanghchaalak or Chief of the RSS, as his view was that freedom struggle must be fought under one organisation that was Congress at that time. He handed over the reins of RSS to Dr. L.V. Paranjape. In his speech, Dr. Paranjape said, "Those who wish to participate in the agitation must do so. Others should work for this young organisation. This current movement is to take our nation forward, there is no doubt. But, this is just one step towards freedom. The real work is to organise such people who will give their lives for the freedom of this nation."[21] *One can see that the RSS leaders had no delusion that this agitation would be the last*. Their goal was to create dedicated swayamsevaks who would be able to stand for the nation for times to come. It was also an option for the young members to choose satyagraha or to keep working for strengthening the organisation that had long-term goals of freedom and reforming the Hindu society.

Dr. Hedgewar left for Pusad on 14th July satyagraha from Nagpur. Speaking to hundreds of people who had gathered to see him off, Doctorji said, "*Please don't be under the impression that this current agitation is the last battle for independence. Real battle will start after this. And be ready to jump into this coming battle fully prepared to sacrifice your all.* We are taking part in this satyagraha because we believe that this will take us one more step towards independence." He was received in every town on way by hundreds of people. Of prominent leaders, Congress leader and Sanghchaalak of Vidarbh Appaji Joshi, editor of Maharashtra's evening edition Balasaheb Dhawle, Dadarao Paramarth, Vitthalrao Dev, Wankhede, Gharote, Bhaiyyaji Kumbalwar, Ambade, Narayanrao Deshpande, Trayambakeswhar Deshpande, Palewar, etc. also went to prison with him.[22] Dr. Hedgewar offered satyagraha in Yavatmal on 21st July. He was handed a nine-month imprisonment with hard labour. Other 11 in that batch received 4 months' imprisonment.[23] There were 100s of swayamsevaks in Akola jail with Dr. Hedgewar. Thousands of swayamsevaks offered satyagraha in other places. Many other prominent RSS leaders offered satyagraha too. Many of these names are mentioned in the biography of Dr. Hedgewar written by N.H. Palkar quoted here, but space doesn't permit me to give all the names and more details.

These satyagrahas by RSS swayamsevaks were also reported in Kesari newspaper dated 20, 22 July, 1930 and 2 August, 1930.[24] After Dr. Hedgewar was imprisoned, number of satyagrahis only increased.[25] This was possible because Dr. Hedgewar was an organiser and motivator par excellence; and organisation he built didn't depend on any leader to deliver. He had set in motion a process of creating a truly cadre based self-driven organisation. We also note that he didn't wish to give false hopes to swayamsevaks after experience of fizzling out of Non-Cooperation movement of 1920.

An important decision by Dr. Hedgewar at that time led to a convention followed by RSS till now. He instructed to work as an organisation of the society, not an organisation within a society. And, RSS members should take part in public programmes as citizens and not as members of RSS. A circular was sent to all the shakhas that 'ordinary swayamsevak can take part in the satyagraha in his personal capacity after taking permission from the local Sanghchaalak'.

RSS and Hindu Mahasabha had their differences from early days. Dr. B.S. Munje wanted RSS to keep away from Non-Cooperation movement. He had been like a mentor of Dr. Hedgewar since his young days. He had helped him a lot in his studies too. But, Dr. Hedgewar politely refused to toe Hindu Mahasabha line and chose his own path in this struggle. Inspite of these differences, Dr. Hedgewar maintained excellent relations with Dr. Munje till last.

In the heated atmosphere of 1931 Non-Cooperation movement, Dr. Munje accepted the invitation for Round Table Conference and got ready for travelling to England. There was strong and bitter reaction to it from supporters of Non-Cooperation movement. Dr. Hedgewar, who was in jail at that time, said, "There can be political differences. But, they should not be exhibited bitterly or cheaply. Inspite of differences, the right way is that each side should respect their patriotism and commitment to the cause and keep working in their own way."[26]

There was a hot debate going on in a meeting about who is better – Gandhi or Savarkar. Asked about his views, Dr. Hedgewar's responded, "This debate is like debating whether Rose is better or Mogra (*Jasminum sambac*). It is a matter of your inclination and choice. At such a time, you should not crush one flower, but enjoy the beauty of each flower that you like."[27] Such was his nature that harmonised different points of view.

Inspite of differences with Hindu Mahasabha, Dr. Hedgewar organised a march past of 500 smartly uniformed RSS swayamsevaks on 30th December, 1935 when HMS held their session in Pune. Dr. Munje himself briefed the delegates about RSS's work as Dr. Hedgewar was not well and had travelled to Pune inspite of strict 'bed rest' instructions from his doctors.[28] It is difficult to think of such affection between organisations holding differing viewpoints in today's fractious politics.

British Watch Over RSS

By 1930s, the British government was worried about growing strength and expansion of RSS. In July 1932, British government file notes – "A development to worry in Nagpur is the work of RSS there. Many of its leaders are involved in anti-government agitations. We need to keep a close watch on this organisation.[29] A notification was sent out in December 1932 in Madhya prant that stopped any direct or indirect contacts with RSS by government servants. "Under Section 23 of government rules for government servants, they should keep away from such a movement." It specifically said, *no government servant should be permitted to become a member or to take part in the activities of RSS*.[30]

Government secretary M.G. Hanlet issued an order on 27th January, 1933 asking the government to collect detailed information about RSS work.[31] Seeing that RSS hadn't bowed down to the ban and was expanding fearlessly, another notification was issued on 20th December, 1933 in Madhya prant. *It noted in the order that RSS was a communal organisation.* Even teachers were banned from attending RSS.[32] We find that 'communal' tag put on RSS by colonialists was exploited and has been exploited till now by Congress and its friends, exhibiting their colonial mindset.

Nashik and Vardha district councils under pressure from British government, too released notices disallowing their employees and teachers taking part in RSS activities. But, with vigorous public contact programme of Dr. Hedgewar, many other Councils passed resolutions opposing such a ban and welcoming RSS work.[33]

March 1934 session of Madhya prant assembly proved to be an eventful session. Dr. Hedgewar had launched a massive personal contact program meeting various Congress leaders and editors of newspapers. The newspapers protested strongly against calling RSS communal and efforts to suppress its activities. Public opinion also began building up against these orders. In this atmosphere, Babasaheb Kolte brought in a cut motion in the assembly. The government was questioned and ridiculed by various speakers. Though there were many factions in Congress, on this issue, *almost all Congress representatives took a strong line in favour of RSS*. They questioned the basis of calling an organisation for Hindus as communal, but not the other organisations who worked for different communities. Mr. Rehman too gave his support to the cut motion, raising questions about definition of communalism. Dr. Hedgewar was present all through in the visitors' gallery, enjoying this spirited debate. Finally, government lost the cut motion, losing its face in the process. Though the government did not withdraw the notification, it just faded away.[34] But, it shows to the length to which British government went and how self-rule elected bodies of Indians fell in line to create difficulties for RSS. It is disturbing that the arguments of Hindu communalism unleashed against RSS by British are still the arguments raised by our political parties that its own leaders had rejected them at that time.

People keep accusing RSS of disrespecting the tricolour. Here is another example of swayamsevaks' loyalty to the tricolour. During the flag-raising ceremony at the Congress Faizpur session of 1937 December, the Congress tricolour was stuck midway on an 80-feet-high mast when Nehruji was unfurling it. Many tried unsuccessfully to untangle the flag, after which a delegate Kishan Singh Pardesi courageously climbed up the mast-pole and freed the flag. People carried him on their shoulders and many people literally showered him with currency notes. The Congress session accepted a proposal to felicitate Pardesi. But no sooner did he reveal that he was a swayamsevak of RSS from Shirpur, Congressmen developed cold feet. When Dr. Hedgewar heard about this contribution of a swayamsevak, he was very happy. While returning from his tour from Nasik, he invited Pardesi to Dhule and publicly felicitated him, presenting a small silver bowl as a token of appreciation and patted him on his back. Dr. Hedgewar said, *"When any act for the nation hits a hurdle, and we have the ability to take it forward, then we should rush forward without thinking about the party, etc."*[35]

Swaraj – Complete Freedom – The Ultimate Aim of RSS

Doctor Hedgewar's commitment to national cause was total, whether it was revolutionary activities or Gandhian non-violent agitations, he supported every patriot. A fact, not much known, is that after murder of Saunders, Rajguru went underground and Dr. Hedgewar made proper arrangements for his underground stay. F.M. Ghodke corroborates this information, "Rajguru is the best example of impact of revolutionaries on Sangh. It was but natural that Doctor (Hedgewar) would help Rajguru in every possible way."[36]

The oath that an RSS Swayamsevak took while becoming an active member of RSS during those days clearly said, "*I will strive for the freedom of this Hindu Rashtra, i.e., Bharat.*" Prof. Rajendra Singh, popularly known as Rajju Bhaiyya, the fourth Sarsanghchaalak, in his audio memoirs notes that the oath contained a line, "I have become a part of Sangh to make Hindu Rashtra free. This sentence, after independence, is now changed to 'for all round development' of Hindu Rashtra. *Objective was clear – to achieve freedom. And after getting freedom, to work as per India's inherent nature and genius, find new ways and not copy west blindly*", notes Rajju Bhaiyya.[37]

Thus, we find that even as RSS was struggling to stand on its feet with its own unique way of organising, Dr. K.B. Hedgewar kept working for freedom of India in every way possible. Because that was his ultimate aim for which he sacrificed his life and created RSS.

❐

Chapter–2
Shri Guruji – A Leader Who Worked Silently

Dr. K.B. Hedgewar left this world at a comparatively young age of only 50 years. He was a very healthy man with imposing physique at one time, but excessive physical strain of moving around and travelling constantly without proper resources including lack of nutrition took its toll and he fell sick, leaving this world on 21st June, 1940. By the time he left RSS in the hands of a young 34-year-old Madhav Sadashiv Golwalkar, popularly addressed as Guruji, RSS had grown well only in Central India (Madhya prant) and adjoining neighbouring districts in Maharashtra. It had registered its presence in only small pockets in other parts of India. However, it was a young sapling as yet.

Nurturing a Tender Plant

Guruji put in his entire energy into growth and expansion of RSS as per directions of the founder of RSS. He began travelling across India relentlessly. Just as he had begun the ambitious expansion programme for RSS with large number of prachaaraks coming forward in 100s leading to all round growth of shakhas across India, the 1942 Quit India movement was announced.

It was a significant and expectedly a very important moment in history of freedom struggle. Young members of this young organisation steeped in patriotic fervour, wished to take part in this movement. But before doing so, Guruji wished to be sure that there was proper planning including proper follow up and back up plans behind this massive agitation. Because a failure compounded by lack of backup plan could mean severe stress on this young organisation that didn't have much of a presence outside the limited geography of two regions. Doctorji too had been circumspect when he took part in 1930 Jungle Satyagraha, having witnessed a sudden culmination of 1921 Non-Cooperation movement in which he had gone to jail.

Support for Quit India Movement on Principles Set by Dr. Hedgewar

After due discussions with his young colleagues, Guruji decided that, *"The agitation is being conducted for the freedom of the country. Therefore, swayamsevaks, as citizens, can take part in this agitation in whichever part of the country they are*. But, as an organisation, Sangh will keep working for national cause, that is organising the society; without getting involved in the agitation directly."[1] This was in line with Dr. Hedgewar's direction during 1930 satyagraha - to work as a common citizen rather than project RSS as a separate organisation.

Sangh, thus, asked swayamsevaks to take part in this national struggle and extend whole-hearted co-operation to it as patriotic citizens. As a result, many swayamsevaks jumped into this battle and took part in it to the best of their abilities as common citizens.

Rajju Bhaiyya corroborates the Sangh support to 1942 and participation of its swayamsevaks in it – "Sangh told that anybody who wishes to take part in this movement should do it in his personal capacity. It should try to help Congress in every possible way that was looking after Hindu society's interest and also work hard to expand Sangh work at high velocity."[2]

Vidarbha region had strong RSS network. Naturally, the most fierce agitations took place in Bali (Amravati), Ashti (Wardha) and Chimur (Chandrapur). News about Chimur agitation was broadcast from Berlin Radio. This agitation was led by Uddhavrao Korekar of Congress; RSS leaders Dada Naik, Baburao Begade and Annaji. A young Swayamsevak, Balaji Raipurkar, was killed brutally in police firing when he was trying to raise the flag to the top. Sangh swayamsevaks took part in Chimur agitation in 1943 alongwith Congress and Tukdoji Maharaj-led Shri Gurudev Seva Mandal.

This encounter became famous in the history of this movement as *'Chimur Ashti episode'. RSS swayamsevaks had established a parallel government in Chimur*. 125 satyagrahis were put on trial and handed imprisonment and thousands of swayamsevaks were imprisoned.[3] Dada Naik was head of RSS Chimur branch. He was sentenced to death. Hindu Mahasabha leader Dr. N.B. Khare, a member of British Viceroy Council, took up his case with the authorities and got the sentence commuted to imprisonment. Later, Sant Tukdoji Maharaj became one of the co-founders of the Vishwa Hindu Parishad.

There was the heroic story of Hemu Kalani of Sakkhar town in Sindh. He was busy removing fishplates from the railway tracks with his colleagues. Their objective was to frustrate the plans to move forces to suppress the struggle in various areas. Unfortunately, Hemu was arrested while his friends managed to escape the police net. Hemu was given death sentence by the Army Court in 1943.[4] Sindhi brethren in Mumbai celebrate the memory of martyr Hemu Kalani to this day. He has a memorial in his name constructed by local Sindhi swayamsevaks and maintained by 'Hemu Kalani Yadgaar Mandal'. This story is also recounted by late Gobind Motwani in his book '9 years of RSS in Sindh – 1939-1947'.[5] Hemu Kalani remains an unsung hero of freedom struggle because Pakistanis won't recognise him as he was a Hindu, while Indian historians won't recognise his contribution probably because he was a swayamsevak. This writer has visited the memorial and has been fortunate to meet many veteran Sindhis in Mumbai who are witness to those days in Sindh, and still active in RSS.

Swayamsevaks plunged into Quit India agitation wherever they were in India and were imprisoned in many places. Some of the well-known senior swayamsevaks were Dr. Anna Saheb Deshpande (Aarvi, Vidarbh), Ramakant Keshav (Babasaheb) Deshpande in Jashpur (Chhattisgarh) who went on to establish Vanvasi Kalyan Ashram, Shri Vasantrao Oak (Prant prachaarak of Delhi), Narayan Singh known as Babuaji in Bihar who later became Bihar Sanghchaalak, and Shri Chandrakant Bhardwaj (who received bullet in his foot that couldn't be removed). Bhardwaj became a famous poet and wrote many poems sung in RSS. There were Madhavrao in East U.P. who became Prant prachaarak later and Dattatreya Gangadhar (aka Bhaiyyaji) Kasture who too became a prachaarak later.[6]

On 11th August 1942, Patna saw a successful attempt by young boys to hoist the Tricolour flag on the government secretariat. Six agitators were felled by police firing. Of these six, two - Devipad Chaudhary and Jagatpati Kumar were swayamsevaks. The first Sanghchaalak of Bihar, Babua ji and senior journalist Krishnakant Ojha confirmed their RSS connection. A felicitation programme to honour them was organised during 50th anniversary celebrations of Independence in 1997 under the Chairmanship of renowned litterateur and revolutionary Shri Vachnesh Tripathi in the presence of the then regional prachaarak, now Sarsanghchaalak, Dr. Mohan Bhagwat. Their kin too were invited in the programme.[6A] There are many swayamsevaks in Bihar who were awarded 'Tamra Patras' as freedom fighters of 1942.

Safe Houses for Underground Leaders

During 1942, oppression by British was in full force. Therefore, people were uneasy about giving shelter to senior underground Congress leaders. At that time, senior high-profile RSS leaders helped the underground leaders of the movement by providing them safe houses.

House of Sanghchaalak of North-West Lala Hansraj was the secret place of stay for Aruna Asaf Ali. She spoke about it in an interview published in Hindi daily 'Hindustan' in August 1967. She said, "I was underground in 1942 agitation, Delhi Sanghchaalak Lala Hansraj provided me refuge in his house for 10-15 days and arranged for my complete safety. He saw to it that nobody got information about my stay at his house. Since underground workers should not stay for long at the same place, I moved out of his house dancing 'Bhangra' in an embroidered ghagra and chunari in a baraat (marriage procession). This dress was given to me by Lalaji's wife. When I went to return it in due course, she refused to take it back, saying, keep it with our best wishes as our gift to you."[7]

"Famous Vedic scholar Pandit Shripad Damodar Satavalekar was the Sanghchaalak of Aundh. He had given asylum for many days to the revolutionary underground leader Nana Patil who had experimented with the novel idea '*Patri Sarkaar*' during this agitation. Nana Patil's colleague

Kisanveer had stayed at the house of Satara Sanghchaalak in Wai while working underground there. Famous socialist leader Achyutrao Patwardhan had stayed at many Sangh swayamsevaks' homes when he was working underground and changed places according to circumstances. Not only had these people, but even the life-long bitter critic of Sangh and a follower of Gandhiji, Sane Guruji used to stay secretly in Pune Sanghchaalak Bhausaheb Deshmukh's house."[8]

A very senior RSS leader shared the story of a swayamsevak, Shri Padsalgikar, who was asked by the state Sanghchaalak Kashinath Pant Limaye to help Vasantdada Patil escape from prison in Sangli. He waited at the spot where Vasantdada reached after breaking out of the jail at 12 in the night. He carried him on his shoulders across fields, nullahs and jungles as all the roads and even village lanes were under police watch. He dropped him off at Vishram Bagh railway station at 2 a.m. so he could catch a train and move out of that area. Padsalgikar, who was a wrestler, went on to become the vice-president of State Kustigir Parishad. He had narrated this story to Dr. Mohan Bhagwat's father at his home when Mohanji was a child. Later, Dr. Mohan Bhagwat, Sarkaryavaah then, met him twice in Sangli and reconfirmed this incident.[8A] There could be scores of such incidents that were never recorded or documented. Since RSS was not keen on documenting or publicising its work as a policy, such inspiring stories are not known outside the local circles.

It would be a good to quote an episode that took place approximately six years later in 1948. Congress committee member of Solapur, Ganesh Bapuji Shinkar took part in the satyagraha to press for the removal of ban on Sangh. He had resigned from Congress on grounds of democratic ethics before joining the satyagraha. He issued a statement clarifying his stand and it was published on 12th December, 1948. He says, "I had participated in Bharat Chhodo (Quit India) movement in 1942. Capitalist and agrarian community was scared of the government at that time. Therefore, we were not offered safe havens in their homes. We had to stay in Sangh workers' homes to work underground. *People from Sangh used to help us happily with our underground work. They also took care of all our requirements. Not only this, if someone from amongst us fell sick, Sangh swayamsevak doctors used to treat us. Sangh swayamsevaks, who were advocates, used to fight our cases fearlessly. Their patriotism and value-based living were undisputable.*"[9]

When anti-national Communists were acting like fifth columnists and getting agitating patriots arrested, Sangh was doing its bit for the struggle. Eventually, the agitation cooled down after 75 days by the end of October. Scattered and weak leadership and disorganised agitation on one side and highly well-entrenched ruling set up of British on the other led to death of a well-intentioned movement in its infancy.[10]

Rajju Bhaiyya, who later on became RSS Chief, noted about 1942 – "I came into Sangh very late. Therefore, there was not much discussion whether Sangh contributed to 1942 movement or not. But, it seems whatever decisions Sangh took was correct. Congress leaders passed the 'Quit India' resolution. All the leaders were caught and put into jail. Not one leader remained out of jail who could guide the nation, the society or the people about the next step. All the big leaders like Nehru ji, Tandon ji and Kripalani ji were members of the working committee. To imagine that the British wouldn't ban Congress or would not send people involved to jails could be excused only as a thinking of a common person with limited short-term thinking. There was no plan for the people who may not have been arrested and were out of prison. Only Ram Manohar Lohia ji and Jayaprakash ji did something outside."[11]

To give a bit of a background, as a young student, Rajju Bhaiyya had very good connections with Congress leaders of that time and as a young man, he would visit Anand Bhavan in Allahabad regularly and seek guidance. Anand Bhavan was the residence of Nehru family and centre of Congress activities in Prayag during 1942 Quit India movement. Lack of long-term planning and organisation resulted in its failure. All the Congress leaders sat back at home, dejected. Rajju bhaiyya met many leaders and asked them about future plans. But, nobody had any clue. He was very disappointed to see this lack of direction in an organisation like Congress. He was studying in final year of M.Sc. It was during this time that he was introduced to Sangh. Rajju bhaiyya confirmed this fact with Shridhar Damle in 1982 when he had gone to America and stayed with him. Two of his friends, Shantaram and Shyamnarayan Shrivastav introduced him to the divisional prachaarak Bapurao Moghe at that time, who was just 5-6 years elder to him. This introduction turned into friendship and Rajju Bhaiyya became a regular Swayamsevak of Bhardwaj sayam shakha.[12] We can, thus, witness a sense of dissatisfaction in the youth of that time about planning and handling of 1942.

We note that wherever RSS had a decent base, its swayamsevaks took part in the 1942 movement enthusiastically. Wherever they could, they helped other participants, thus strengthening the movement in every possible way.

Relations between RSS and Hindu Mahasabha

Reader will recall that Dr. Hedgewar had differences with Dr. Munje in 1930s about Non-Cooperation movement, and how he maintained cordial relations with Hindu

Mahasabha (HMS) inspite of these differences just as he kept good relations with all the patriots and organisations. We see differences of the same type cropping up in 1942 between HMS and RSS yet again. Though they were on the same page on many issues and supported each other, but some differences did crop up once in a while.

The earlier HMS leaders prior to Savarkar were expecting that the RSS would work as a 'youth organisation' of the 'parent body'. But that expectation did not materialise and HMS under Savarkar's leadership was forced to form the Ram Sena in its place. Hindu Mahasabha was not in favour of taking part in 1942 for various reasons, which were more to do with their more militant approach against the British. They were interested in using the World War II to gain military training for the Hindu society and nurture fighting spirit. At that time, Savarkar preferred to tour India asking Hindu youth to join the military with a call '*Militarise the Hindus, Hinduise the nation*'.[13] However, we also saw that Dr. Khare fought for RSS swayamsevaks in Chimur Ashti cases.

HMS had put pressure on RSS to stay away from the Quit India movement but RSS took a decision to support 1942 Quit India movement. For this, HMS was critical of RSS. This unhappiness simmered for a long time, but cooled down over time. Shri Guruji maintained good relations with Veer Savarkar. Savarkar invited him in the concluding session of Abhinav Bharat in 1952 in Pune where it was dissolved as its goal of independence had been fulfilled.[14]

There is an interesting sidelight. Veer Savarkar's younger brother, Narayan Savarkar, was the first Sanghchaalak of Mumbai RSS when it opened its branch in 1934 in Mumbai. He was also a member of HMS and went to jail in 1921 during Non-Cooperation movement. Arya Samaj used to be another very active Hindu organisation in Punjab. Most of Arya Samaj activists slowly gravitated towards RSS over time.

British Eyes on RSS

During this period, the British rulers were alert and cautious about RSS. They had kept a sharp eye on every activity of Guruji. The British tried to curtail Sangh work in various ways. For example, it sent out a directive. *Under its part 56-58, it banned military uniform and army education by private organisations. It did not mention RSS by name, but it was clear who was the target.* It was in line with its earlier attempts in 1932 and 1933 to suppress RSS mentioned in previous chapter. Shri Guruji circumvented this order by sending out letters that indicated changes in its uniform, its official designations and training syllabus.[15] CID kept sending reports about him regularly.

The British Intelligence reported that on 27 April, 1942, at the training camp of the RSS at Pune "*Golwalkar condemned those who were selfishly helping the British Government*… On 28 April, 1942, he declared that the Sangh has resolved to do its duty even if the whole world goes against it and impressed on the volunteers that they must be ready to sacrifice their lives for the cause of the country."[16]

A report of the Home Department shows the anti-British nature prevailing at the RSS camp at *Jubbalpore* (Jabalpur) where a speaker proclaimed that the aim of the Sangh was to drive the British out of India and the sentiment was repeated by other speakers.[17]

A CID report noted, "Membership of Sangh is swelling continuously. In Central Province, membership has increased from thirty-two thousand to thirty-three thousand three hundred forty-four. It has reached twenty thousand four hundred seventy-six from eighteen thousand twenty nine in Mumbai and fourteen thousand from ten thousand in Punjab.....We can see the recent well-spread-out tour of the present Chief of Sangh, M.S. Golwalkar as an example of such efforts. In the last month of April, he was in Ahmedabad; in May, he was in Amravati and Pune. In June, he was in Nasik and Benaras. He toured Chaandaa in August, Pune in September, Madras and Central Province in October, and Rawalpindi in November."[18]

Another CID report dated 30 November, 1943 – "Golwalkar has told volunteers in a training camp in Madhya Pradesh that the training is being given to experience army life and *that time is coming fast when we will have to test our strength against those foreigners who have given lot of pain to Hindu society*.[19]

The report on 30 November, 1943 notes, "Rashtriya Swayamsevak Sangh is moving ahead rapidly towards building a highly significant all-India organisation. Spokesmen of Sangh keep saying that the basic goal of Sangh is to achieve Hindu unity..... it is clear that Sangh is bent upon expanding its area of influence and *this year it has been able to bring on board, the famous religious saint Sant Tukadoji Maharaj* from Central Province for spreading its message."[20]

The following extracts from a CID report also gives a glimpse about the intelligence gathering skills of British and their keen understanding of Hindu-Muslim politics. It is a matter of conjecture now how history would have evolved if the Congress leaders were as insightful as British about Islamist politics.

Report dated 13 December, 1943 shows that British intelligence was wary of Shri Guruji's work. It says, "It is not possible to create a case for banning Sangh. But, it is equally clear that Golwalkar is creating a strong organisation at a rapid pace that would obey the orders, maintaining confidentiality and jump into any activity of sabotage or of any other type whenever required as per their leader's orders. The structure of this organisation looks superficially like that of '*Khaaksaars*'. But, *the fundamental difference between the two is that the leader of Khaaksaar, Inaayatullah, is a big-mouthed imbalanced lunatic, while Golwalkar is a very cautious, crafty and much more capable leader.*" CID report further cautioned, "*Though seen on superficial way, the danger posed by Golwalkar's activities is still quite far off, but to give him an opportunity to establish himself as uncontested leader of a rebellious group out to destroy peace with its action, by letting it grow with uncontrolled speed into a powerful disciplined volunteer organisation would be taking an unnecessary risk.*"[20A]

The noting of Home Department official G.A. Ahmed, in this report unravels the government's real intention: "the holding of all camps by any organisation whatever should be prohibited by an order under the Defence of India Rules. This will hit the RSS most, as its main activity is the organisation of camps." Subsequently, the Sangh's training camps were raided and literature and arms were seized, besides the arrest of organisers. This 1943 report of the intelligence department on RSS said in most clear terms: "*The ulterior objective of the RSS is to drive away the British from India and free the country.*"

We see that inspite of various government circulars in different states threatening legal action against the government servants and teachers who attended RSS shakha, RSS work kept growing. *It is also clear that British were no friends of RSS*. As the British report points out above, Guruji proved a smart and intelligent leader who could not be stopped with legal stratagems. He circumvented the legal loopholes to keep working and expanding RSS network, even as many of swayamsevaks were active in 1942. Oppression of RSS, though, did not stop.

Various Contributing Factors to the Final Decision of British to Quit India

It seems that people and the history writers of that period have different perception about impact of 1942 movement on achieving freedom for India. It is true that it was the last mass movement before India attained freedom in 1947. However, we must not forget that revolutionaries were active during the entire period of independence movement beginning in 1857 and did not let British enjoy their rule unperturbed and undisturbed.

Indian National Army (INA) action under the leadership of Netaji Subhash Chandra Bose during World War II and subsequent Naval Rebellion in early 1946 were telling blows to British imperialism. The rebellion showed that the British rule was no more held in awe. Various writings of pro-Congress or Left historians seem to have given more than due weightage to 1942 movement, while discounting the above two developments during the fag end of the freedom struggle. They concluded that 1942 was a major cause for departure of British from India. We can be more objective with benefit of hindsight now.

In all, there were three mass movements for independence– 1921, 1930, 1942; each about 10 years apart. One must salute the commitment of people of India and their mass participation in Quit India. It was unparalleled. However, analysing objectively, 1942 cannot be the sole criterion for certifying people as freedom fighters and brushing off the contribution of those who struggled for freedom in their own way during this historic period of sustained resistance to foreign rule.

By 1945, the Second World War had ended. The allied powers led by Britain and the United States had won. The axis powers led by Hitler's Germany had been vanquished. The victors wanted to impose justice on the defeated armies. In India, officers of Netaji Bose's Indian National Army were put on trial for treason, torture, murder. This series of court-martials came to be known as the Red Fort Trials.

Indians serving in the British armed forces were inflamed by the Red Fort Trials. In February 1946, almost 20,000 sailors of the Royal Indian Navy serving on 78 ships mutinied against the Empire. They went around Mumbai with portraits of Netaji and forced the British to shout Jai Hind and other INA slogans. The rebels brought down the Union Jack on their ships and refused to obey their British masters. This mutiny was followed by similar rebellions in the Royal Indian Air Force and also in the British Indian Army units in Jabalpur. The British were terrified. After the Second World War, 2.5 million Indian soldiers were being de-commissioned from the British Army.

Military intelligence reports in 1946 indicated that the Indian soldiers were inflamed and could not be relied upon to obey their British officers. There were only 40,000 British troops in India at the time. Most were eager to go home and in no mood to fight the 2.5 million battle hardened Indian soldiers who were being demobilised. It is under these circumstances that the British decided to grant independence to India.[21]

R.C. Majumdar says, "... and *it was effect of all three that got India independence. Out of these, the facts that came out, it is that the INA trials led to huge reaction in India. Due to this, British whose morale was already broken due to the World War, realised that she cannot depend on loyalty of soldiers to rule India. This was possibly the biggest reason for them to leave India.*[22]

We need to understand that there were more forces at work for India's independence and there were more factors leading to independence than what our established historians would want us to believe. ❐

Chapter–3

15th August 1947 Did Not Herald Independence for All the Indians

When the Congress leaders boast of gaining independence for India, they forget two things. One, as we have seen above, it was a cumulative effect of many a factor, and supported by people of all shades of opinion under an umbrella organisation named Congress. Two, they want us to forget that when process of freedom was set in motion around 1946, Congress leaders thought their job was over and got busy with the formalities of taking over the government.

When Partition was agreed upon, Congress leaders did not foresee the violent aftermath that would be unleashed. We cannot impute that they were naïve as they were wise men and women. However, it does seem that they did not worry too much about it as subsequent developments show. In fact, most of Congress leaders on the western side of the partition (proposed Pakistan) were one of the earliest ones to escape the violence and come to newly truncated India; many times taking help of RSS.

The violent upheaval and trail of disaster left behind by the partition was handled from civil society side by RSS at a heavy cost to its swayamsevaks and leaders. This tragic and violent history is paid a lip service, but the onus of this tragedy and insensitive handling of the victims of this violence is not put on anyone nor talked about much. Naturally, the yeoman service rendered by RSS is also not remembered nor RSS credited for doing what should have been a natural duty of a new government and the supposedly biggest organisation, that is, Congress that had agreed to partition.

For the victims of this violence, declaration of independence was not the end of a chapter, but the beginning of a terrible nightmare. And in this nightmare, it was RSS that held the candle of hope.

Weakness of Congress Leadership in Wake of Muslim League Promoted Violence

It is important to lay bare some unpalatable truths of that period. To quote Ranga Hari, "The period of 1946 to 1947 August-September was violent tragedy for India. Mohammad Ali Jinnah, by now the uncontested leader of Muslim League, had got a resolution passed on 23rd March, 1940 in Lahore session with the demand "Cut Hindustan into pieces and hand us over our Pakistan." On the other side were great Congress leaders of the time – Gandhi-Nehru-Patel. Jinnah was accepted as the official spokesperson of this community. On this side, Hindu community accepted Gandhi-Nehru-Patel triumvirate as its leaders, ignoring Hindu Mahasabha and its leader Savarkar. These three leaders had earned the confidence of nearly the entire Hindu society. The third actor, Lord Mountbatten exploited this politics by playing the two against each other, enjoying his power. As subsequent events would show, he was acting with clear intent of creating a permanent headache for India by subtly siding with Pakistan on issue of Kashmir."

"In 1946, Congress had passed a resolution that it stood for United (Akhand) Bharat. Iron man Sardar Patel had roared that 'sword will be met with sword'. Jawaharlal Nehru's pet song was 'Pakistan is a fantastic nonsense'. Mahatma Gandhi had written in 'Harijan' on 6.4.1947 and 13.4.1947, "*Two-nation theory is a baseless falsehood. My conscience abhors this very idea. .... Division of Bharat is a scenario that is worse than anarchy. It is unbearable chopping-off of limbs. Cut me down before you divide Bharat.*" These words had a huge impact on people. Populace had put their faith in leaders whom they looked upon as angels due to their selfless sacrifice throughout their lives to the cause of freedom. But, Muslim League waved its 'green flag' for 'Direct Action' on 16th August, 1946 and Muslims butchered thousands of Hindus mercilessly, with indescribable cruelty. Congress was shaken to the core due to this act. Congress showed bankruptcy of the '*kshatriya*' spirit of putting up a fight and not running away from battle-ground."[1]

Thus, path of freedom had lot of land mines in the form of violence perpetrated on the very nation and the people who were supposed to get freedom by peaceful means. As history unfolded, the plight of displaced Hindu, Sikh and other brethren became a major tragedy for the nation during the twilight period that did not end on 15th August, 1947. The dark shadows of twilight period stretched beyond it for many more months.

Project Freedom was not yet over. RSS understood this and stood firm to dispel the darkness to whatever extent it could. However, this dark chapter of freedom struggle is not paid enough attention by official historians.

RSS – Standing Firmly with Hindu-Sikh Brethren

Guruji took up the responsibility of keeping morale of common people high in these difficult times. He also sent message across to people to conserve their energies, build up their strength to face the looming disaster ahead. Criticising this 'weakness in action' of the leadership at that time in his speech during the Vijayadashami festival on 5th October of 1946, he said, "Arjun had suddenly faced a mesmerising dilemma when his chariot stood between the forces of Kauravas and Pandavas. There stood before him Gurus, brothers, fathers and sons. Arjun was not a coward, he was brave. He did not wish to run away from the battle field, but wished to lay down his life by dropping his arms and turning his face away from worldly affairs pleading '*nivritti*'. Our nation is facing the same situation today. Like Arjun, Hindu society finds itself mesmerised with the dilemma of action versus non-action, doing duty or not doing duty."[2]

On another occasion, he noted, "There is a lot of talk about not picking up arms and not taking revenge. But, I cannot agree with this current language of not reacting; it is not something arising out of bravery. It is nothing but cowardice and about fooling ourselves. *It is 'adharma', that is, immoral to inflict pain upon self.*"[3] Appealing to be ready for self-defence, he affirmed unhesitatingly, "It is our firm belief that every individual has a natural right to self-protection and the society made of such individuals also has the same right. I had read a bizarre statement in newspapers, which said, 'An individual or society does not have the right to defend self, only the government has this right, and a person should not take law unto his hands even if he is attacked.' Only Law has the right to defend an individual and society. Does it mean that we should sit quietly and wait for police if somebody attacks us? Should there be no attempt for self-defence? How far can this be justified? *Right of self-defence is a right endowed by nature to every individual and society.*"[4] This, perhaps, was another reason for Congress to dislike RSS, as it refused to show the other cheek and submit meekly.

Prominent leaders of RSS including Guruji, Babasaheb Apte and Balasaheb Deoras travelled extensively in the troubled areas. Hindu brethren started coming together with self-confidence in cities and villages of Punjab like Rawalpindi, Lahore, Peshawar, Amritsar, Jalandhar, Ambala, etc. English Tribune wrote, "Punjab is the sword arm of Hindustan and R.S.S. is the sword arm of Punjab...*Perturbed with this development, mouthpiece of Muslim League, Dawn, wrote, "If Congress leadership wishes to receive co-operation from Muslims, then it must ban Sangh immediately."*[5] This desperate comment by Muslim League supporters shows how frustrated were the Muslim goons baying for Hindu blood during partition. It also shows ignorance of Congress about the ground situation and cowardice against an aggressive political grouping that was out to destroy the nation with its violent character, ready to go to any extent to achieve its objective.

RSS's Faith in Congress leadership

During his tour of Punjab in November 1946, District Sanghchaalak, Dr. Baldev Burman asked Guruji, "There is lot of noise about Pakistan. Is there a possibility that it might be created?" Revered Guruji replied, "I have full faith in Mahatma Gandhi. He will never agree to this proposal of Pakistan. It is possible that he may agree to many of Jinnah's proposals to appease Muslims. But, he will never allow partition of the country."[6] Such was the faith and respect Guruji had for Gandhiji!

Not Competition, Full Support to Congress

Around this time, Pandit Nehru had reached Hyderabad in Sindh. Muslim League supporters had decided to sabotage Nehru's meeting and had conveyed their threat too. League members felt that Nehru will definitely oppose the demand for Pakistan. Therefore, they had decided not to allow his meeting. Local Congress leaders became restless when they got this information. Their two senior leaders Chimandasji and Baba Kisanji met city Sanghchaalak Hotchandji and asked for Sangh's support and co-operation for a trouble-free meeting. Sanghchaalak agreed with open heart. Many swayamsevaks attended this meeting accordingly. Finding RSS swayamsevaks in Congress meeting, League ruffian's condition was like mice who had seen cats amongst them. Meeting got over peacefully without any trouble.[7]

In Amritsar, RSS swayamsevaks rushed into a burning bungalow of Radhakrishna Seth, a Congress leader, to save his four daughters. The house was covered from all sides by Muslim League goons before putting it on fire. While other family members had managed to escape but these girls could not. Radhakrishnaji later told Nehru, "Sangh is not a group of mindless youth, but an organisation of ready-to-save-the-nation patriotic youth."[7A]

Hindu support for a united, *akhand* Bharat was unwavering. Ranga Hari notes that common Hindu populace was not in favour of partition even after Jinnah's 'Direct Action'. *Communist Party was in favour of partition and supported* Muslim League. It had passed a resolution in favour of partition. At the same time, British rulers and other leaders were planning for partition of the country in the background.

Under a political settlement, a coalition government of Congress and Muslim League was formed in Delhi in September 1946. Central Assembly (called Parliament now) went into session with this arrangement. League began throwing tantrums immediately. First day witnessed unruly scenes both inside and outside the assembly. Goonda power of Muslim League showed its true colours. They decided to play this game with utter contempt even on the second day. But, leaders had decided not to allow this insulting behaviour to be repeated. To put this idea in place, top leader of Delhi state Congress, Lala Deshbandhu Gupta came to Sangh office in Kamla Nagar and met state prachaarak Vasantrao Oke. As a result of these talks, hundreds of swayamsevaks surrounded the Assembly hall since the morning to give a strong response to this ruffian behaviour. Sensing adverse conditions on the ground, the goons lost their nerves and assembly carried on with its session in a dignified manner. Inspite of all this, partition of our Motherland was announced on 3rd June, 1947.[8]

These incidences show that RSS carried neither animosity nor had any competitive feeling against Congress. It was its firm conviction that Congress represented all Indians of various view-points for the purpose of independence struggle and it went to any extent to support this struggle.

RSS to the Fore

Condition of Hindus became precarious in the disturbing circumstances where Muslim League goons went on violent rampage. Great exponents of non-violence turned silent witnesses. RSS under the leadership of Guruji reached out and set up Punjab Relief Committee and Hindu Sahaayata Samiti. Lahore was the centre of activity for both of these. Punjab state Sanghchaalak Raibahadur Badridas was the Chairman and Dr. Gokulchand Narang was the Treasurer of these committees.[9] As the requirements increased, nearly all the districts had relief committee branches manned by RSS swayamsevaks.

In a letter published in Punjab Kesari on 31st May, 1982, Sardar Harvansh Singh ji shared his experience about how RSS Swayamsevak stood as human barriers on 4th March, 1947 when Muslim League goondas began rioting and tried to attack Hari Mandir Sahib as most of the Hindu-Sikh brethren were away in Anandpur Sahib to celebrate Hola Mohalla. When the attack began at 1 pm, he with his friends rushed to Durbar Sahib chowk. He found 50 swayamsevaks holding fort there in uniform. They had swords and two guns. They assured that more swayamsevaks were ready in different areas of Amritsar. Bijli Pahalwan was informed and he sent trucks and collected 8,000 armed villagers by 8 p.m. to save Amritsar. Till this time, swayamsevaks held on and defended the Bijli Chowk. No Muslim goon dared to cross it. This incident has been republished in *Jyoti Jala Nij Pran Ki*.[10]

These riots in Amritsar lasted six months and had reached every nook and cranny of Amritsar's lanes. They were triggered by Muslim League after full preparations on 5th March, 1947. Ultimately, Hindu society overcame this challenge under the leadership of RSS swayamsevaks.[11] This writer's own maternal uncle, a swayamsevak, nearly lost his life as he lay posing dead on the street with other bodies. He lost one of his fingers and partial hearing in these riots.

There were two RSS training camps from 16th to 20th July, 1947 in Phagwara and Sangrur, in which attendance was 1,400 and 2,300, respectively. It had sizeable number of Sikh brethren too. Guruji went to visit these camps. Members of Gurudwara committee of the holy Mastuanaa sahib Gurudwara visited the training camp to invite Guruji to the Gurudwara. Many Jathedaars (heads) of Gurudwaras of Pepsu region had also been invited. Chief of the Gurudwara said, "*It is our immense fortune that we have a great soul amongst us today who has tied the sacred thread of protection akin to Sikh arm gear – kadaa for defending dharma. He is raising a strong force with power of his meditation that will surely defend dharma.*" He was offered '*saropaa*' (a sacred piece of cloth blessed by Shri Guru Granth sahib) after his short speech. Expressing his gratitude, Guruji said, "As I witness this scene before me, I recall a page from three-hundred-year-old history, when the great Bharatiya power of North in the form of Guru Gobind Singhji had tried to meet another similar power that had risen in South, Chhatrapati Shivaji. But, it is a misfortune for this nation that they could not come together. The meeting that couldn't take place then is happening today. I firmly believe that we shall see the rise of an immense power in defence of dharma that will leave no doubt about any threat to our dharma in future."[12] Such was the close bond between Sikhs and Hindus, whom Sangh addressed as Keshdharis and Sahajdharis of the same larger Hindu society who had different faiths.

Rashtra Sevika Samiti founder and its Sanghchaalika at that time, Smt. Laxmibai Kelkar, popularly called Vandaneeya Mausiji visited Karachi with her colleague Venutai on 4th August 1947. They were the only two women in the flight. Shri Jayaprakash Narayan was in the same flight and got down at Ahmedabad. Anti-India slogans ranted the air with shouts like "*Lad ke liya Pakistan, hans ke lenge Hindustan*". Violence had gone out of control. Names of the roads were being changed, so also the language. In these troubled times, Hindu New year festival was celebrated in Karachi, where around 1,200 sevikas (members) were present. Crux of Mausiji 's lecture was, "Have courage, keep faith in organisation and keep serving your motherland. These are testing times," and raised their morale. Many ladies feared that their honour was at stake. She told them to be like Durga. She also assured them that arrangements will be made for their safe travel to Bharat. Many families and women were brought to Bharat. Those who were facing warrants of arrest were kept in safe Mumbai homes in complete secrecy.[12A] Such was the courageous spirit of women of Sangh school of thought. Sheela Kripalani and Jethi Dewani of Rashtra Sevika Samiti rendered valuable help to Hindus in Sindh at that time.[13]

RSS Swayamsevaks on the Front to Save Jammu & Kashmir

'*Jyoti Jala Nij Pran Ki*' is a well-documented book with eye witness accounts of resistance of swayamsevaks and other Hindus and atrocities of Pakistani forces in the guise of kabailis (tribals) on women. It gives town-and village-wise eye witness accounts from Srinagar to Mirpur, Alibeg, Kotli, Rajouri, Poonchh, Skardu, Dev Batala, Udhampur, Akhnoor and Jammu. Swayamsevaks worked hard with other villagers to prepare an airstrip in Punchh to help air force and army there. They fought shoulder to shoulder with army and helped it in familiarising it with local geography by accompanying it in the above places.

When Pakistani attack in Jammu and Kashmir began, RSS workers fought valiantly, organised villages and towns for resistance. Stories abound in the book in chapter 5 about Jammu and Kashmir. This book is too small to give all the details but suffice to say if one were to take into account, various episodes of bravery described in the book, number of swayamsevaks who sacrificed their lives, the number would go to hundreds. For example, Ramkishen Datta was eye witness to the happenings in Mirpur. He talks of days of resistance put in by Hindus led by swayamsevaks in Mirpur to keep Pakistani army and their frontmen kabailis (tribals) at bay.[14]

Pandit Premnath Dogra, an important public figure, had become Sanghchaalak of Jammu-Kashmir division (vibhag) of RSS in 1941. He played a key role of resistance against Pakistani aggression. He headed Purusharthi Sahaayata Samiti in 1947-48 that was organised by RSS to provide relief to displaced Hindus and Sikhs escaping from Pakistan via Jammu, Lakhanpur and West Punjab. Pandit Dogra later organised and led the Praja Parishad that struggled hard for complete accession of J&K with India and fought against two flags, two constitutions under Article 370. This agitation was hugely successful in Jammu and had full RSS support.[15] This agitation played a key role in integrating Jammu and Kashmir with India and implementation of Indian Constitution in J&K and ended with arrest of Sheikh Abdullah.

On 14th August, 1947, the postal authorities in Srinagar hoisted the Pakistani flag on all their offices reasoning that the post offices within the State came under Sialkot circle which now formed part of Pakistan. Promptly, the Sangh swayamsevaks under the leadership of Jagdish Abrol and Prof. Balraj Madhok got hundreds of tricolours made in RSS office and went out together to replace all the Pakistani flags at one go. They then appealed to all the citizens of Srinagar to hoist the Indian flag. More flags were prepared overnight in RSS office and entire Srinagar was awash with Indian tricolours.[16]

On October 5, 1947, Pattan in Kotli was attacked. Maharaja's army's Muslim soldiers joined enemy camp. Hindus of Kotli tried to defend Kotli, setting up 26 fronts of which army jawans manned 8 while swayamsevaks manned 18 fronts, with 70-75 swayamsevaks on each of them. When

Palandhari was attacked, a team of swayamsevaks with army went to protect it. It included senior swayamsevaks like Master Manoharlal, Bakshi Krishanlal, Lala Jargar Singh, Pandit Raj Bakshi, Durgadas, Dwarkanath and Laxmichand, etc. Of these, only Bastiram, Thakurdas and Lalsingh Jargar survived to tell the tale, all others were martyred, killed in cold blood by tribal commander Diler Khan.[17]

Another hair-raising story in Kotli is about 16 swayamsevaks under the leadership of RSS city secretary, Vedprakash who crawled into the midst of enemy territory facing fire to pick up 12 boxes of ammunition and medicine air dropped for army. Six of them died while bringing back the boxes. The six were Vedprakash Chadda, Dharmveer Gupt, Kalaram Jargar, Somraj Kohli, Surajprakash and Amritlal of Sarsawan. Their bodies were taken out in huge procession and last rites were done in the sounds of booming military gun salutes.[18]

When the Indian army landed in Srinagar and a group was to advance to Poonchh, enemy burnt down the wooden bridge. Sixty swayamsevaks under the guidance of senior RSS worker Amritsagar went there to create a diversion within 3 hours.[19] Swayamsevaks and refugees under leadership of Amritsagar also helped the army in creation of a runway in Poonchh within 72 hours, cutting trees, bringing down government houses. It included Master Moolraj Sharma, Sardar Kubersingh, Master Beliram, Gyani Jeevan Singh, Gyani Thakur Singh, Babu Biharilal, Sardar Gopichand Thekedar, Munshilal, etc. This enabled landing of 35 aircrafts every day and evacuate 40,000 people.[20]

The vibhag prachaarak of RSS at that time for Jammu & Kashmir, Shri Jagdish Abrol, led these campaigns courageously from the front throughout this entire period.

Prof. Balraj Madhok, one of the senior workers played key role in the resistance at that time and went on to become one of the founders of Bharatiya Jan Sangh.

Guruji's Role in Accession of Jammu & Kashmir

There is an almost forgotten chapter about Shri Guruji's role in accession of Jammu and Kashmir to India. He had paid personal visit in October 1947 to persuade the Maharaja to accede to India. He never believed in publicity or broadcasting the work of Sangh. He believed that serving one's motherland is a natural duty and need not be news.

Guruji kept receiving all this information from time to time about the merger talks from the RSS karyakartas who had good relations with the Maharaja. He decided to go to Srinagar. He reached Delhi by air on October 17, 1947 with Delhi state prachaarak Vasantrao Oke and Barrister Narendrajeet Singh. Regional prachaarak of that area-Madhavrao Muley and 4-5 state, level workers of Jammu-Kashmir were waiting for them.

As per Sangh's arrangement, Guruji and his colleagues stayed in Barrister's in-law's home in Divaaniyat Bhavan. Next day, on October 18, Guruji went in a private car to Karn Mahal to meet Maharaja. Maharaja and Maharani had great reverence for Guruji. So, both of them were there at the palace gates to receive and welcome him. After initial informal chat, formal discussions began at 10.30 a.m. Nobody was present from both sides during these discussions. So, nobody knows what exactly transpired during the discussion, what kind of suggestions came up. When Maharaja came out to bid farewell to Guruji after the discussions, he came near his car and said, "I will definitely weigh your suggestions carefully." Before leaving, Guruji urged Maharaja, "It may be a good idea to send Prince to Jammu and you should remain in Shrinagar so people's morale should not dip." Guruji and his colleagues reached their lodging before lunch."[21]

This incident was corroborated in a signed statement by Captain Diwan Singh who was his ADC at that time and remained Maharaja's ADC till his death. He passed away in 2016. This document has been published in the book *Shri Guruji aur Jammu-Kashmir*, edited and compiled by well-known historian Dr. Maharajkrishna Bharat and published as a commemorative volume by Shri Guruji Janmashatabdi Samaroh Samiti. Late B. N. Varhadpande was present during this meeting and he described meeting and discussions during the time in monthly magazine, Tawi Deepika published from Jammu in October 1988.[22]

In the book, titled 'India: Shedding the Past, Embracing the Future, 1906-2017', Arun Bhatnagar, a 1966 batch IAS officer, who is considered a close aide of Sonia Gandhi and effectively ran her brainchild National Advisory Council (NAC) writes that on October 17, 1947, at union home minister Sardar Vallabh Bhai Patel's instance, Guru Golwalkar flew to Srinagar to explain to the Maharaja the futility of entertaining ideas about Jammu & Kashmir's independence. The Maharaja expressed willingness to sign the Instrument of Accession in favour of the Dominion of India, which was reported to Sardar Patel. However, the invasion of the State by tribesmen from the Pakistan side in the next few days altered the situation completely. Maharaja Hari Singh had to seek urgent military aid from Pundit Jawaharlal Nehru cabinet but the cabinet refused to send Indian troops unless the Maharaja acceded, arguing that the Indian Army could only defend Indian territory.[23]

That same evening there was a pre-planned get-together (saanghik) of senior swayamsevaks in DAV College in Mangal

Bagh near Lal Chowk that was attended by more than 500 volunteers. Guruji delivered his 'bouddhik' (discourse). He did not speak anything about his meeting with Maharaja. He returned to Delhi on 19th October. Guruji met Home Minister Sardar Patel in Delhi and apprised him of favourable attitude of Maharaja. Fortunately, Meharchand Mahajan had become the 'Prime Minister' by that time in place of Ramchandra Kak. Finally, Jammu-Kashmir merged with the rest of the country.[24]

Last Man Standing

Guruji toured Punjab and Sindh repeatedly during 1943 to 1947. *Guruji's final tour of Sindh took place just one week before partition on August 7, 1947.* That day, 35,000 out of the 65,000 population of Hyderabad city came to National College grounds and heard Guruji with rapt attention. Two days before this, Karachi had witnessed a massive public meeting. This meeting, overflowing with people at Fire Brigade ground, was presided over by great spiritual personality Sadhu T.L. Vaswani. Common man of Sindh had sensed the coming partition by then and everybody knew that this was the Guruji's last visit to Sindh.

It is a noteworthy fact from historical perspective that people's hero, Guruji, was the last leader to tour united Bharat's Sindh to be with Hindu brethren till the end, that is, seven days before partition. By then, the so-called other great wise leaders of Sindh had escaped to safe destinations.[25]

Guruji instructed a team of top RSS workers to stay behind to give legal and moral support till the issues of Sindhi brethren were resolved and then return to India. This team consisted of Jhamatmal Wadhwani, Hari Atmaram Samtani, Hashu Advani, Lachhman Matai, Narain Bhavnani and some other swayamsevaks. This intrepid team stayed back for nearly a year in Karachi after partition! RSS prachaarak Rajpal Puri was their leader and made Jodhpur his centre to guide the rehabilitation process, where Kishan Murari had made arrangements for him in Rajput Sabha Bhavan.[26] There were separate teams of Sindhi swayamsevaks who worked out rehabilitation plans. By 1948, about 11 lakh out of 13 lakh Sindhis had reached India. Swayamsevaks of RSS welcomed and served them to the best of their abilities.[27]

Relief Work for Displaced Brethren

Sangh established *Purusharthi Sahayta Samiti* under the Chairmanship of Pandit Premnath Dogra in 1947-48 that opened refugee relief camps from Jammu to Lakhanpur for refugees coming from West Punjab.[28]

Bastuhara Sahaayata Samiti was formed in Kolkata. Its branch was opened in Guwahati in another three weeks. Help poured in. Rupees 8,56,687 was collected in funds and 1,500 bales of cloth were received. One fist full of grains (Mushti Ann) plan was floated and helped thousands of displaced Hindus in overcoming hunger. In Assam, centres were opened in Pandu, Shillong, Silchar, Tinsukia, Dibrugarh and Agartala. Later on, more centres were opened in Nagaon, Tejpur, Dhubri, Lamading and Karimganj. Efforts were also made to get over hate campaign launched by vested interest between Bengali, Assamese, hill and plains' citizens, Ahoms and non-Ahoms, etc. and focus on relief and peace. Swayamsevaks were active in border villages for immediate support to harassed and tired refugees. Displaced people were brought to relief camps after initial help and given 'Refugee Card'. This card had such reliability that even government relief agencies honoured them. This work was carried on for one month, till government took over the management of relief work.[29]

Punjab Relief Committee was formed in March 1946 when robbed and harassed Hindus from West and North-West states in Punjab began to come to Lahore and were housed in refugee camps. Many had escaped with only three pieces of clothes on them. Hindus and Sikhs contributed with open hearts. New clothes, medicines and grains came in large quantities. People helped with large heart as and when a call went out from the committee. All this was being done with the help of young disciplined swayamsevaks when cities were seeing 70 hours curfews.[30] According to A.N. Bali, Hindus and Sikhs had begun coming to Lahore. Relief work was being organised mainly by RSS swayamsevaks. These people would stay for a few days in these camps and move out to their relatives in Haridwar, Dehradun and Delhi, etc.[31]

These relief camps run by RSS played a saviour's role for the homeless, violated and robbed brethren of Punjab, Sindh, Jammu & Kashmir and Bengal.

Standing by Hindus against Razaakars' Violence

Scenario in Hyderabad in South was very different from Kashmir in North. Nizam of Hyderabad's intention was to declare independence, get recognition from U.N.O. and then become a part of Pakistan. Maharaja had not provoked minority Hindus to exploit majority Muslims in Kashmir. But Nizam of Hyderabad organised minority Muslims as *Razaakars* to terrorise majority Hindus day in and night out. Neighbouring state of Central Province had to worry about protecting the helpless population from human devils. Both Chief Minister Ravi Shankar Shukla and Home Minister Dwarika Prasad Mishra sought Guruji's co-operation. Guruji put them in touch with the Vidarbh Sanghchaalak Bapusaheb Sohoni. Sohoniji writes about this episode thus, "We planned a major drive in Washim, Mehkar, etc., areas when Razaakars were running riot. Purpose of our campaign was to generate confidence in the people, banish their terror and generate confidence in people about government's ability to protect their life and property. Government provided us with petrol and other facilities."[32]

RSS – The Saviour

Writing about those terrifying times of partition, Professor A.N. Bali, in his book 'Now It Can Be Told' says, "*Who came to the rescue in those difficult times for protection of the people, except those young men known as RSS?* They arranged for safe passage of women and children in each and every mohalla, in every city of the state. They arranged for their food, medical help and clothing and took their care in every possible way. They organised fire-fighting teams in different cities and towns. They arranged for lorries and buses to carry escaping Hindus and Sikhs and posted defence teams in railway trains. They patrolled relentlessly in different Hindu and Sikh localities. They trained people in self-defence. They were the first ones to reach these terrified people, first to help them and were last to come to secure places in East Punjab. *I can recount the names of many well-known Congress leaders in different districts of Punjab who took help from RSS for their own security and security of their families. They (RSS swayamsevaks) never ignored any call for help. There were many cases where Sangh volunteers took Muslim women and children from Hindu mohallas to Muslim League refugee camps.*"[33]

A.N. Bali describes terrible conditions that the displaced brethren faced in various centres government had created to help them, and how they were seething in anger. He highlights the cold-minded cynical logic of bureaucracy running the government for whom refugees formed only 3 per cent of the population, making no sense in putting other 97 per cent in difficulty by fighting with Pakistan.[34] He goes on to contend, "If it were left to Sanghis alone, the problem of rehabilitation of refugees from West and East Pakistan would have been solved long ago."[35]

Ranga Hari quotes from the above-referred book, "When entire Punjab was on fire and Congress leaders were sitting helplessly in Delhi, at that time, volunteers of RSS saved people of Punjab with their discipline, physical strength, risking their own lives. Now, if somebody from outside Punjab was to tell Hindus and Sikhs to forget those Sikhs and the brave heroes' action from Rashtriya Swayamsevak Sangh, who put their lives at risk to defend them, then their calls would go unheeded."....*Each and every person from amongst refugees who came from West Pakistan is indebted to Sangh. When everybody had abandoned them, only Sangh stood by them.*"[36]

Sardar Patel in his reply to a letter by Shri Guruji dated 11-08-1948 accepted, "There is no doubt that Rashtriya Swayamsevak Sangh served the Hindu society during its moments of crises. Youth of Sangh worked hard to secure lives of women and children in areas where it was required. *But, I believe that people from Sangh can do their patriotic work only in collaboration with Congress.*"[37]

K.M. Munshi in Akashwani weekly dated 2-10-1949 noted on page 6-7, "In the unfortunate days of nation's partition, youth of Sangh showed extraordinary courage in Punjab and Sindh. *These youth saved honour and lives of thousands of women and children. Many youth lost their lives performing their duty.*[38]

There were examples of RSS swayamsevaks who got 'sunnat' done, learnt Islamic practices, and infiltrated Muslim League ranks. One of the examples is of two youths – Charanjit of Jammu and Omprakash of Gurdaspur in Jalandhar. Sunnat was done by Dr. Jitendra Singh, an RSS Swayamsevak.[39] They infiltrated Muslim League ranks to get gather intelligence. *Jyoti Jala Nij Pran Ki* also refers to presence of Sikhs in large numbers in RSS ranks during this time, many of whom lost their lives saving their brethren. One of the brave Sikh RSS workers named in the book is Sardar Pradyumn Singh who was kaaryavaah (secretary) of a shakha in Lahore in Badami Bagh.[40]

Dr. Kamal Kishore who was a student of Lahore Medical College shared his experience about swayamsevaks who formed a team to cremate bodies. They would be so busy that sometimes they would not get time to eat. As soon as the news came, they would rush to that area to take the body for cremation and reach back the family safely to their homes. Dr. R.N. Kataria (a surgeon in Delhi later) and Mahendra were in charge of this activity. He told that many a times, they would have to make arrangements for 10 bodies in a day. Another swayamsevak Chunilal told about a time when flooded Ravi river didn't allow them to reach the cremation grounds. They took the bodies in a truck from Mayo hospital to dispose them off in the flooded river. Chunilal was made the chief of Mansevi camp. Many RSS swayamsevaks worked with him. There was a network of such relief camps in Taran Taaran, Patti, Khemkaran, Attari, Ajnala, Dera Baba Nanak, etc. These were extended to Pathankot, Gurdaspur, Hoshiarpur, Abohar, Firozpur, Jalalabad, Muktsar, Jind, Talwandi, Fazilka, Ambala, Jalandhar, and Gurgaon, etc. on the east Punjab side too.[41]

From 15th March to 10th October nearly 300,000 people were helped. There were 20 relief camps. These camps also helped Muslims. *Nearly 30,000 Muslims were not only taken care of with food and medical care, but were provided help in crossing over safely across Kathua border.*[42]

A senior member of RSS at that time, Vaidya Amarnath Dogra talks of an incident when Bhimsen Sachchar, a big leader of Congress, was threatened by Muslim goons. When Sangh people came to know about this, they put 4-4 swayamsevaks for entire day for his security. When he came to know about it after 10-15 days, he went to thank RSS workers, who said it was just part of their duty."[43] I will talk later about how he paid back for this selfless service.

This book tells us about brave resistance to Muslim goons during riots related to partition, including Sikhs like Pradyumn Singh, Tara Singh and Tilakraj, Mahendra, etc. who were killed in riots or bullets of Baloch army. Such was the faith of common people that they would reach out to swayamsevaks rather than police in case of any problem. Authors provide many names and incidents narrated by witnesses of those times.[44] There are hair-raising and heart breaking stories that speak of the sheer audacity of swayamsevaks during these disastrous times.

Suffice to say that RSS swayamsevaks played a major role in fighting off the Muslim League goondas and also seeing to it that Hindu-Sikh families reach India safely. One shudders to think how many thousands would have been sacrificed at the altar of partition had RSS not intervened.

Naturally, popularity of RSS was growing hugely during this time. This led to heartburn among Congress leaders, particularly Pandit Nehru, who got worried that RSS may pose a challenge to Congress.

Ranga Hariji in his biography of Guruji, notes, "Tireless efforts put in by Sangh to resettle the refugees properly could not be overlooked by anyone even if one wished to. However, in political circles, this generated jealousy and dread. Responding to it pointedly, Guruji had noted in the Vijayaadashami festival of that year on 24th October, 1947, "Reacting to the acknowledgement that Sangh has received for easing the pain of affected Hindu people of Punjab, an English daily has commented that it is 'unfortunate, but true.' Various political parties also wish to confront Sangh in a similar manner. *They are worried that in case Sangh enters the arena of electoral politics, what will be their fate. I wish to assure these parties trying to save their respective reputations with means fair or foul, that their fear is meaningless.*"[45]

Duty Towards Motherland is Not News

In the same public meeting, in order that swayamsevaks and friends of Sangh keep a right perspective, he clarified, "Swayamsevaks provided whole-hearted support to the people in that horrifying situation. For this, *Sangh has never appreciated its swayamsevaks because Sangh swayamsevaks have only done their natural duty.* Just as a brother taking care of his sick brother, keeping awake by his bedside doesn't get details of his services published in newspapers, similarly, swayamsevaks have served their brethren and helped them. Therefore, we didn't feel need to sing paeans to them."[46]

Gandhiji and RSS

Mahatma Gandhi was staying in Harijan basti during this period. Harijan brethren had built a small but beautiful and clean temple for their forefather, the effulgent soul Sage Valmiki, in one corner of the colony. On the other side, there was a large settlement of Muslims. Therefore, government had acknowledged internally that Mahatma's life was not safe in that Harijan settlement. Gandhiji, on the other hand, was against posting of military or police for his security there. In this state of dilemma, top *Congress leader, Krishnan Nair met state prachaarak, Vasantrao Oke and requested him to arrange for security of revered Bapuji. Vasantrao implemented a proper plan for this.*[47]

Mahatma Gandhi showed his interest in addressing the RSS swayamsevaks during these days. An urgent rally was organised and *Gandhiji addressed the swayamsevaks on 16 September, 1947*. This episode is recorded in 'Sampoorna Gandhi Vangmaya'. In this lecture, he recalled his earlier visit to RSS shakha in Vardha where he had gone with Jamnalal Bajaj. He said firmly that he was a Sanaatani Hindu. At the end, he said, "Sangh is a highly well-organised and disciplined organisation. Its strength can be used for the good of Bharat or against it. I do not know if the accusations against Sangh are true or not. It is up to Sangh to prove such accusations wrong with its good work."[48]

15th August did not Mean that the Job was Over

While the nation celebrated Independence, RSS was on its toe to safeguard India's newfound freedom. Bharat Ratna Dr. Bhagwandas noted, "Not even thirty days had passed since proclamation of independence when Muslim League hatched a conspiracy to blow up the top leaders of Bharat. They had made plans for a massive explosion in September 1947. Alert swayamsevaks working day and night had done their own investigation and passed on precise information to Sardar Patel. Based on this information, armed forces raided many places in Paharganj and surrounding areas and captured large cache of arms and explosives, and took action against the rebels." He further notes, "I have confirmed information that some Sangh swayamsevaks of Delhi had gone to the extent of making a show of accepting Islam to gain trust of Muslim League members in order to get details of the conspiracy hatched by them.... The conspiracy of 10th September was to kill all the ministers and civil officers and thousands of Hindu citizens, unfurl Pakistan's flag on Red Fort and grab control of Indian government.... *If these young men, fired by ardour and patriotic feelings, had not provided information about this conspiracy in time, there would have been no Indian government today.*"[49]

We find that at this critical juncture of history, top leaders of Congress were busy with administration and ministry-making, many Congress leaders were already enjoying ministerial powers in provincial governments after 1946 elections and rest were busy in celebrating the dawn of independence. *But, they forgot or closed their eyes to the misery faced by orphans of partition and brutalities perpetrated on millions at that time. At that moment in history, RSS put in all its efforts to minimise the pain of victims of partition for whom independence had brought nothing but devastation and penury.*

Many people allege that RSS did not reconcile to Partition and was very critical. Yes, it is true. But, to understand the reason of this feeling, one needs to read what RSS Sarsanghchaalak felt about displaced persons of partition. Guruji had gone to Amritsar in September 1947. Justice Ramlalji and social leader Meharchand Mahajanji came there to meet him. They began by saying, "Guruji, after all, we are refugees." On hearing these words, Guruji said immediately, "No, you are not refugees. This nation belongs to each and every individual. All of you have same rights over her. *How can somebody be a 'refugee' in one's own home?*"[50] This view of Guruji was the reflection of his unshakeable faith that, "Bharat is one, unbreakable (*akhand*) and all her citizens are children of this unified nation." Even later, whenever he heard somebody use the word 'refugee' or 'sharanaarthi', his face would twist into a pained expression as if somebody had uttered foul language. Guruji's view was that if an unfortunate brother has to come into the loving fold of a fellow brother, how can he be a refugee? Is serving or supporting him an act of charity? Then, how can we talk of love and affection? What is the meaning of duty? We should look at our brethren of our society with a feeling of brotherhood and love. He felt that only those people who don't have this sentiment about their unfortunate brethren can call them refugees. This word is an obscenity to insult those unfortunate fellow beings. Such was his heartfelt view of the situation.[51]

Our historians and RSS critics have failed to appreciate that the struggle of freedom did not end with drawing of lines across India's map to partition it and lowering of the Union Jack. People paid a heavy price for this political haste and short-sightedness of leaders of that time. RSS and its swayamsevaks stood steadfast on the frontlines to provide succor to our unfortunate Indian brethren. This truth is not just negated or brushed aside, it is not even acknowledged in historical records.

It was not just Guruji, many other savants of the time felt the same way about the independence and partition. Maharshi Aurobindo spoke resoundingly against the partition. It would be, therefore, interesting to quote from his famous Independence Day Message of 15 August, 1947: "India is free but she has not achieved unity, only a fissured and broken freedom..... It is to be hoped that the Congress and the nation will not accept the settled fact as forever settled or as anything more than a temporary expedient. For if it lasts, India may be seriously weakened, even crippled.... the partition of the country must go – it is to be hoped by a slackening of tension, by a progressive understanding of the need of peace and concord, by the constant necessity of common and concerted action, even of an instrument of union for that purpose. In this way, unity may come about under whatever form – the exact form may have a pragmatic but not a fundamental importance. But by whatever means, the division must and will go. For without it, the destiny of India might be seriously impaired and even frustrated. But that must not be."[52]

The Post Script to Proclamation of Independent India: *Liberation of Forgotten Territories of Goa, Daman, Diu, Dadra and Nagar Haveli, and Pondicherry*

Sadly, after independence, the Congress rulers virtually forgot about Portuguese enclaves of Goa, Daman, Diu and Dadra and Nagar Haveli, and French enclave of Pondicherry (now Puducherry) But, RSS did not. Its swayamsevaks took part in liberation of Goa and other Portuguese enclaves with full support from the organisation. These enclaves were finally liberated in 1961 from the Portuguese officially. Since we are talking about events leading to the independence of India from British, I will be brief about this part of history, because without mentioning them, the history of independence cannot be complete. Let us know a little about the role of RSS here in this struggle.

One of the early catalysts for the liberation struggle was Dr. Ram Manohar Lohia. Then, in the early 1954, RSS volunteers Raja Wakankar and Nana Kajrekar visited the area around Dadra and Nagar Haveli, and Daman several times to study the topography and get acquainted with locals who wanted the area to become part of India. In April 1954, the RSS formed a coalition with the National Movement Liberation Organisation (NMLO), and the Azad Gomantak Dal (AGD) for the annexation of Dadra and Nagar Haveli into the Republic of India.[53]

On 2nd August, 1954, a team of 100 swayamsevaks led by Vinayak Rao Apte, Sanghchaalak of Pune stormed the enclaves of Dadra and Nagar Haveli. Then, they attacked Silvassa, forcing 175 Portuguese soldiers to surrender and national tricolour was hoisted and handed over to the Central government. This were felicitated on 2nd August, 1979 in Silvassa.[54]

In 1955, RSS leaders demanded the end of Portuguese rule in Goa and its integration into India. When Prime Minister Jawaharlal Nehru refused to provide an armed intervention, RSS leader Jagannath Rao Joshi led the satyagraha with a group of around 3,000 members straight into Goa. He was imprisoned with his followers by the Portuguese police. Non-violent protests continued but were met with repression. On 15 August, 1955, the Portuguese police opened fire on the satyagrahis killing thirty or so civilians.[55] Rajabhau Mahakal of Ujjain led the batch from Ujjain. He died in the police firing while he held the tricolour aloft even after a bullet had pierced through right eye.[56] Jagannath Rao Joshi was one of the prominent leaders of Jan Sangh later in Karnataka.

These freedom fighters were not treated with sincerity and respect they deserved. Mohan Ranade and his friends had led the revolutionary armed struggle in Goa under the banner of Azad Gomantak Dal. Mohan Ranade and his colleague Telu Mescarenus remained imprisoned in Goa and later in various Portuguese jails till 1969. They were released thanks to sustained efforts of Shri Sudhir Phadke, the famous music director and a swayamsevak.[57] Mohan Ranade in his memoirs 'Sarfaroshi ki Tamanna' tells us how badly he suffered due to apathy of Nehru government and subsequent Congress governments. This book also confirms that Nehru disapproved of various patriotic efforts to liberate of these enclaves.[58] He confirms participation of RSS swayamsevaks in this struggle. Indian and French parliaments finally ratified the treaty of cession only on 16th August, 1962 for Pondicherry, when it joined the Indian Union. It is a serious indictment of our political leadership that while India attained freedom in 1947, millions of its inhabitants remained slaves in enclaves surrounded by the mainland India.

❒

Chapter–4

Political Envy and Partisanship Leads to Targeting of RSS

It is important to explain the build-up to the ban on RSS and to show that Gandhiji's assassination was just an excuse for banning RSS. This will help readers understand why the Congress-Left propaganda mills are still churning out the same old stale falsehood. I will not ask who benefited most from this killing and who suffered the most. The answer is obvious. I will not even ask why no action was taken to secure Gandhiji life inspite of Madanlal Pahwa's confession about the conspiracy to kill Gandhiji barely ten days before this dastardly act. Recall that he was caught after his failed attempt to bomb the prarthana sabha of Gandhiji. I don't want to fathom the reason why a post-mortem was not done, a normal procedure in case of such unfortunate death. Readers can ponder over these issues and analyse this horrific incident checking other historical records available in public domain now.

I just wish to let people understand the mentality behind creation of this anti-RSS environment. Ideas to crush RSS to destroy any possible competition to Congress monopoly on power in future were already being tried. RSS popularity in this period was at its peak. The reward for all the good work of RSS that put its volunteers to severe risk to save the people from marauders and help them resettle was ingratitude from the ruling party that had failed in its duty to protect the citizens of this country, vivisected to gain freedom. In any other nation, such brave citizens would have been rewarded and feted. This ill-will sprung from the envy and jealousy of some Congress leaders (not all). But, these few leaders were at the top and they dictated the Congress policy of hate against selfless patriotic RSS. Through these powerful leaders, this sense of animosity percolated down to mid-level leaders who felt insecure with the rising popularity of RSS.

It needs to be remembered that Gandhiji had advocated dissolution of Congress to let multiple parties rise out of its ashes with different ideologies and ideas. But, the top Congress leadership wanted to encash the brand created by freedom struggle in which the entire nation and people from all shades of ideology had contributed. Therefore, it was instinctively opposed to any other political idea or formation striking roots in Indian soil.

Senior RSS thinker Ranga Hari, in his biography of Shri Guruji, documents a few of such attempts of Congress to stall RSS growth. Reader must not lose sight of the fact that all this happened before the assassination of Gandhiji. Campaign to somehow crush RSS was already on.

Congress Leaders Out to Suppress RSS

According to daily 'Dainik Kaal' dated October 13, 1947, Satara Congress committee in Maharashtra passed a resolution and asked Chief Minister B.G. Kher to '*Uproot Rashtriya Swayamsevak Sangh*'. In a threatening tone, the committee claimed that 'otherwise we would destroy Sangh ourselves using 1942 type of terrorist methods'. Giving sagely advice to them, Chief Minister told them, "Don't take up an action in a mood of pessimism, or else you would be totally destroyed."[1]

It was decided to hold a full-fledged camp of young swayamsevaks of Western Maharashtra in Pune on November 1-2, 1947. One lakh swayamsevaks were expected to attend this camp. Being trained and habituated to volunteer for Sangh work, swayamsevaks took leave from their jobs and businesses to make arrangements for the camp in sufficient numbers. Guruji's presence throughout the period of the camp was assured. Sardar Patel had agreed to come as the Chief Guest. Aakashwani (All India Radio) had also arranged for broadcasting the news about the camp. Support from all quarters for the camp was available as expected. There was an atmosphere of enthusiasm all around. But, there were evil souls, feeling uncomfortable and seething with jealousy in Congress camp. Ultimately, the state home minister gave an excuse of a grave situation and rescinded the permission for the camp. It was clear that Sangh had become victim of internal pulls and pressures within Congress.

In reality, there was not a trace of disturbance anywhere. Therefore, swayamsevaks were more angered than disappointed. Any programme for protests and condemnation would have been successful. But, senior Sangh workers decided to convert this curse into a boon. Guruji sent out a notification immediately that there would be big rallies (saanghik) in full Sangh uniform in each district of Maharashtra and Guruji would be present in each of this get-together. Anger of swayamsevaks was transformed into zeal, and they began working with a strong will to succeed. Guruji toured all the thirteen districts from October 24 to November 5. When the final reports were prepared, it turned out that more than 400,000 swayamsevaks from 1,300 villages and towns had attended these programmes.[2] This is how RSS responds to calumny and negativity.

This incident indicated the direction in which Congress government's mind and machinery were moving. Next month, in November, a meeting of Chief Ministers was called in Delhi. The topic of discussion was increasing popularity of Sangh and challenge arising out of it. The problem facing them was how to bridle Sangh.[3]

Around this time, accusing swayamsevaks of fomenting riots in Kandaale in Uttar Pradesh, the Congress government there put up cases against them. These accusations were proven incorrect later on and they had to be released. Such evil designs were witnessed in other places also.[4]

Later on, there was a meeting of *All India Congress Committee on 17th January, 1948 in Delhi that passed a strongly worded resolution against Sangh. It demanded state governments also to take anti-Sangh steps.* Lowest units of Congress were asked to follow this policy. During this time, Central government also released a circular that said, "It was illegal for a government servant to be a member of RSS." Leader of this anti-Sangh front was Uttar Pradesh minister Rafi Ahmed Kidwai.[5]

Imagine the disappointment of swayamsevaks that all this was happening in the backdrop of massive service to the nation undertaken by the swayamsevaks in the wake of the Partition.

Prof. A.N. Bali noted, "They (Sangh) were considered the saviours of the people and it was a universal belief that they had made the rehabilitation of a part of the Hindu Sikh refugees possible in East Punjab. ....Pandit Nehru's government has utterly failed so far to rehabilitate the few lakhs who became its direct charge. *Pandit Jawaharlal Nehru in his Cawnpur speech has accused the Sangh of creating disturbances in Punjab without adducing any proof....* But a person in his responsible position should have carefully weighed his words before uttering them.[6]....Their discipline, their physical fitness and their selflessness is face of dangers came to the rescue of the people in Punjab when the whole province was burning and when the Congress leaders were helplessly fiddling in New Delhi, not being able to overcome the opposition of the Muslim League and the obstinacy of the Governor-General to their proposal for stronger action for the maintenance of Law & Order.[7]

RSS – Victim of Internal Politics of Congress

Madhya Pradesh's home minister Pandit Dwarika Prasad Mishra made a statement that seemed to be in favour of Sangh. Countering the allegations of the opposing camp, to Nagpur Navbhaarat (19th December, 1947), he said, "The very idea that Sangh can overthrow government on the strength of lathis is laughable. It is surprising that this allegation was not made against the local D.S.P. *I cannot believe at all that Sangh is a political organisation and that there is a possibility of it overthrowing Pandit Nehru's government.*"[8]

While newly independent nation was passing through a grave crisis, diverse pulls and pressures and tensions between Nehru-Patel came into open. Even Sangh had to suffer because of this. Speaking in a public meeting on 6th *January, 1948, Sardar Patel had said, "Congress people in power should behave in a different way with Sangh rather than laying stress on their own rights and powers. It is not possible to suppress an organisation with the power of penal action. Sangh people are not the type who will fight for selfish interests. They are patriots who love their motherland."* Within a few days, Pandit Nehru, as if in response to this speech, spoke in Amritsar, "Sangh and Hindu Mahasabha people have insulted our national flag. They are traitors. I will crush them."[9]

Thus, there were voices of dissonance in governance. Once in safe confines of partitioned India, many Congress leaders changed their tune including those who had sought RSS help to reach India. One striking example is that of senior Congress leader, Shri Bhimsen Sachchar mentioned earlier, whose house was secured by RSS swayamsevaks in Lahore. He went on to blame RSS for Gandhi murder without any evidence; and his government in Punjab was in forefront in torturing swayamsevaks jailed during satyagraha for lifting the ban. This writer came to know about the torture also from his own two uncles who were jailed during the satyagraha.

Objective Voices in Media

Approach and analysis of newspapers about persecution of RSS was objective. They did not agree with government blindly. Daily 'Hitavaad' wrote on October 28, "Sangh has limitless capacity to unite and organise Hindu society and take it above narrow emotions of caste, sect and language...... people who see germs of Hitler's Nazi organisation in Sangh, are making a grave mistake."[10]

Vaartaa Vihaar of North Karnataka and South Maharashtra published the public speech of 'Karnataka Kesari' Gangadhar Rao Deshpande after another six days on 25th December, 1947. In this speech, he had said, "Congress has passed a resolution recently very cleverly against Sangh.... *strange are the games of fate that as soon as they got hold of power, they are parroting the idea of 'do not organise' whenever they think of Sangh....* But, looking back at my experience of past 50 years, I can state not once but again and again, that organising Hindu is very crucial for maintaining peace in our country.....I pray to the people in power not to shirk away from this organisation. This organisation will ultimately come to their rescue at a crucial time."[11]

Most strident editorial appeared in Tribune from Delhi. The editor wrote on November 26, "*Pandit Nehru has instructed East Punjab government to ban RSS and Akali Dal and destroy them. This news is so dreadful that it should not be true at all. And if it is true, then it can only be termed as a misfortune of this country……Because it is necessary for us to remind Pandit Nehru that if these nationalist organisations had not faced the cruel and inhuman Pakistanis with their bravery, then thousands of Hindu and Sikh sisters would have been raped, thousands of Sikh and Hindu children would have been butchered………..*we wish to say this with full force at our command that Sangh and Akali Dal have made a place for themselves deep in the hearts of the people of this bordering state. Populace there looks at them as the sentinels of their state….. It is nothing but ingratitude to brand these organisations communal or private armies. In fact, they are nationalist powers out to help us who have discipline like army, but have no arms. Indian government should be proud of them."[12]

Congress leadership never expected backlash of this magnitude. They kept quiet for some time, but they were looking for the right opportunity. The real reason for this was pointed out by Shri Banahatti, the moving spirit of Sarvoday movement, in his weekly 'Savdhaan'. He wrote openly, "In this period, Rashtriya Swayamsevak Sangh is the only organisation that can challenge Congress. *Talented, dedicated young class of high character is getting attracted to Sangh due to its organised strength. This is the reason Sangh has become an eye sore for Congress leaders.* Congress is taking the nationwide work of Sangh, its impact on educated, intelligent youth and rare qualities like readiness of its swayamsevaks to work patiently in times of any disaster as a challenge to itself. Growth of same spiritual qualities in Sangh due to which Congress used to think of itself as a superior power; is making Congress uncomfortable."[13]

One can clearly see a pattern in the Congress efforts at harassing RSS and crushing it over the preceding months. Congress government was bent upon not letting RSS any avenue to grow. It did not wish to let young disciplined men help rebuilding a nation that recently got independence and was ravaged by partition with and pain of displaced people who had lost their all.

It was waiting with an evil intention for the right opportunity 'sooner or later' to disrupt the sustained, unbroken *tapasya* (meditation) of Sangh. Just at that time, *billi ke bhaag se chheenka toota*' (pot broke down to the great fortune of cat). Unfortunate assassination of Mahatma Gandhi provided them this opportunity.

RSS Responds Sharply to Gandhiji's Assassination

It is educative to see how RSS leadership responded immediately to this ghastly act. Reaction of RSS was that of shock and revulsion. Some of the phrases used by Shri Guruji in his communications were – *'a despicable beastly act' and 'feeling of extreme revulsion and grief'. He called the act 'unpardonable and anti-national'. RSS shakhas were suspended for 13 days as a sign of grief and condolence, an unprecedented act in RSS history.* Given below is sequence of events that unravelled after the assassination and quick and sharp response of RSS.

Guruji was in the midst of a meeting in Chennai when he received the news of Gandhiji's assassination. He was to leave for Vijayawada the same night by G.T. Express, but he cancelled the plan immediately and got busy sending telegrams or letters to the concerned people. He sent separate condolence messages to Prime Minister, Deputy Prime Minister, Gandhiji's son Devdas Gandhi.[14]

Advocate Rajagopalachari's chamber was converted to an ad-hoc central office that night. Messages were typed out and instructions sent to concerned centres. On the same date, Sarsanghchaalak passed instructions from Chennai to all the shakhas, "To express our grief due to sad demise of respected Mahatmaji, shakhas will observe condolence period for 13 days and all daily programmes will be put on hold." Guruji left for Nagpur on Saturday, 31st December by air.[15] *This suspension of shakha work was never done till that time, nor was it done later even on death of its most cherished top leaders, including Shri Guruji.*

Immediately upon reaching Nagpur, on 31st January, the same day, Guruji wrote to 'Respected Panditji' in English and 'Maanyavar Sardar ji' in Hindi. Apart from difference in language, contents and import of both the letters was same. In the letter sent to Patel, he wrote, "I was in Chennai yesterday when I heard about the tragic news that has shaken the whole humanity. Such an evil and condemnable incident would never have taken place in history. Heart is distressed with unbearable pain.... It is difficult to find right words to condemn the person who has carried out this despicable act. One cannot even think of such a senseless evil act. What can one say of a person who has stunned the whole world into silence?"[16]

Guruji released his press statement on the first day of February for publication in newspapers. He had prefaced his statement thus, "Assassination of the most revered and popular supreme personality of the modern world is a despicable, a beastly act of the worst kind. At such a time, leaving aside our tradition of not giving public lectures and statements, I feel that it is my duty to express the feeling of extreme revulsion and grief that has engulfed my heart.... Today, situation of our country is precarious. *At such a time, presence of that person of unity and peace was acutely required. Murder of such a great personality is an unpardonable anti-national act.* Our heart is enraged when we think of the harm that our nation has suffered and we are worried about future." In such a severely tragic scenario, while requesting people to take the path of service, he told swayamsevaks, "If somebody speaks with irresponsibility due to irritation or passion, or somebody exhibits unnecessary fury, even then Swayamsevak brothers should understand that this is an expression of love and respect of every citizen for the Mahatma who raised prestige of our nation in the eyes of the world." This statement was sent out for publication to the news agency A.P.A. The agency didn't release it in full but released it in a twisted form. Many newspapers simply overlooked it. Organiser of Delhi published it in full. But, it was merely a weekly with limited circulation.[17]

Congress Exploits the Tragedy

The preconceived agenda reflected in the speeches of so many Congress leaders and acts of oppression were put into motion. Home Minister of Central Province at that time, Dwarika Prasad Mishra wrote in his autobiography, 'Living in an Era', "*Mahatma Gandhi's assassination gave a handle to unscrupulous politicians to defame and, if possible, to pull down their rivals is difficult to deny.*"[18]

'Dawn' supported by Pakistan's ruling party published it fully that highlighted the ban on Sangh with a remark that betrayed its sense of satisfaction that, "*Our old demand had been fulfilled today*."[19] Readers will recall that in the previous chapter, I quoted The Dawn, asking for a ban on RSS during the violent days of pre-independence. This statement is indicative of the hate and fear Islamists had about RSS. It is ironic that the interests of Pakistanis matched the interests of RSS critics at that time just as they match in the present times.

Shri Guruji was arrested immediately after Gandhiji's assassination on draconian charges Sections 302, 307 and 120.[20] Later, Sections 302 and 120 had to be dropped as the government realised its mistake in overarching ambition to corner RSS. But, he was put under 6 months of detention under Defence of India Act.[21] *Even though a CID report clearly stated that RSS had no role in killing of Gandhiji within a month of the incident, this report was never disclosed,*[22] and charade of "RSS killed Gandhiji" was carried on for months. Home minister Patel had written a long letter based on this report to Nehru on 27th February, 1948. This was a classified document but now available in Patel Nehru correspondence and this letter is on page 56-57. *It stated that the news of distribution of sweets and celebrating Gandhiji's murder was wrong, and that RSS was not part of the conspiracy. This disclosure tells us that both Patel and Nehru knew the truth 5 months before Guruji wrote to them asking for the proof of RSS's hand in Gandhiji's assassination or lifting of the ban.*[23] It shows that reason for the ban lay elsewhere as indicated by their attempts at browbeating RSS much before this tragedy.

Neither the court nor the conspirators named RSS, nor did the final judgement name RSS. Repeated demands of RSS leadership to produce evidence against it or drop charges and lift the ban went unchallenged. All that government could do was to make vague baseless charges.

According to A.N. Bali, the government of India struck strongly and mercilessly after Mahatma Gandhi's death at the workers of Hindu Mahasabha and the Sangh. According to a report published in the New Delhi paper 'the Hindustan Times', as many as ten thousand persons were arrested in the country after Mahatmaji's assassination, ...*A mass hysteria overtook the non-violent Congress workers and supporters. According to government's own admission in the Parliament, as many as 1,000 houses were burnt or razed to the ground, hundreds of people attacked, killed or injured in Maharashtra and the rest of the country.*[24] In this seminal work written in 1949, he also mentions how RSS satyagrahis in jail were treated cruelly and provided with sub-human facilities.

How Sangh fought the ban peacefully, how this ban was removed after lots of political games played by the Congress leadership is not the topic of this book. Suffice to say that after grim fight back through peaceful satyagraha, the ban was lifted. Satyagraha of Rashtriya Swayamsevak Sangh ran for 45 days from December 9, 1948 to January 22, 1949. As per last count, number of satyagrahis was 77,090. Incidentally, this figure was bigger than number of prisoners held during 1942 agitation that was recognised as the biggest mass movement for independence.[25] There was not a single instance of violence inspite of police atrocities in many places across India and very poor jail conditions. Congress party was so perturbed by this satyagraha that the UP government in addition to taking disciplinary action against government servants also declared that *watching of such demonstrations would amount to a gesture or expressing of sympathy with the RSS rendering them liable to department action.*[26]

Government could not prove any charge against RSS but kept up the farce of ban giving specious reasons. The final excuse was that RSS had no written constitution. Ironic fact was that even Congress didn't have a written Constitution for nearly 14 years after its birth. There were no other conditions. The ban was lifted unconditionally upon RSS presenting a written Constitution to the government. This Constitution was nothing but a document that presented RSS principles it was professing openly and working methodology that it had been actually practicing all these years.

Unconditional Lifting of Ban

I end this part by quoting Shri Guruji himself in his response to questions raised about some so-called conditions for withdrawal of the ban. There was a felicitation on 28th July, 1949 by Nagpur University and another public felicitation on 29th July. Editor of Hitavaad newspaper, A.D. Mani, wished to know during his felicitation speech about so-called conditions of government and assurance by Sangh. Guruji expressed his views in his acceptance speech, "I had wished to keep silent on this issue about me giving a written assurance to the government... I can definitely say this to you that at that time I was not speaking as Golwalkar – an individual – but as a representative of a nationally spread out massive organisation. *For the organisation, on whose behalf I was speaking, I would have given up my life before it was insulted; but would never have allowed it to be insulted. I wish to assure you that I have not given any acceptance or assurance of any type.* I can just clarify that reaching an agreement means that both sides take a step back. With this view, on advice of respected T.V.R. Shastri, I gave my permission to put in writing the way Sangh work was being conducted for years. Shri Shastriji is elder by a year to my father. I had given this permission in deference to his prestige and knowledge. ....That Sangh to whom you look up with such love and sense of hope, for that Sangh I have not spoken or written even a word that could result in an insult to it."[27]

Still this matter raised lot of smoke and dust for nearly two-and-a-half months after the ban was lifted. A legislator from Surat, Shri Lallubhai Makanji Patel submitted a list of questions in Maharashtra assembly. Following is the detailed questionnaire:

1. "Will honourable Home and Revenue minister please let us know:
2. Is it true that ban on Rashtriya Swayamsevak Sangh has been lifted?
3. If it is so, what are the reasons for removing this ban?
4. Has the ban been removed with some conditions or without any condition?
5. If it has been removed conditionally, what are those conditions?
6. Has government been given any assurances by the leader of Rashtriya Swayamsevak Sangh?
7. If so, what are these assurances?

Shri Morarji Desai's answer on behalf of Shri Dinkar Rao N. Desai was:

- ✓ Yes
- ✓ Ban has been lifted because it was not found necessary to continue it in future.
- ✓ It was removed without any conditions.
- ✓ Such a question doesn't arise.
- ✓ No
- ✓ Question doesn't arise."[28]

These responses should silence the critics who tell us that there were conditions attached to lift the ban on RSS. The talk of RSS promising to keep away from politics as a condition to lift ban deserves no refutation as I have noted in previous chapter that RSS Sarsanghchaalak had reiterated it clearly even before issue of ban came up, that RSS was not interested in entering political arena.

❐

Conclusion

This small compendium of facts should conclusively prove that RSS, a young organisation at the time of freedom struggle, played its role in this struggle to the best of its ability. Its members took part in 1930 and 1942 agitations for freedom struggle, while its founder took part in freedom movement in various ways since young days including 1921 agitation before RSS was born.

More importantly, its members stood up boldly to protect the citizens of this nation to the best of its ability at a heavy cost to self. They stood boldly to save millions of brethren from the fires of partition and rehabilitate them from 1946 till after political independence announced on 15th August, 1947. RSS swayamsevaks stood firmly in Jammu and Kashmir to save it from Pakistani attack in 1947 and worked towards its accession with India.

RSS was wedded to the cause of Swaraj or complete freedom from its inception. Dr. Hedgewar had illustrated this urge time and again. Oath that swayamsevaks took clearly mentioned struggle for freedom. It was preparing men to fight for freedom. British records show that they were vary of RSS using its growing clout. To convert this freedom into Swaraj meant India required disciplined and brave spirited young men who would be dedicated to the national cause. So, it carried on its man-making mission even while many of its swayamsevaks took active participation in agitations.

Movement for freedom did not end with 'Tryst with Destiny' on 15th August, 1947. There were endless dark nights in this twilight period, when RSS workers were the biggest organised force apart from security forces who put their lives to risk to salvage whatever they could, of destroyed lives of millions. To protect their unfortunate brethren, they had to pick up arms too, for which they were pilloried as communal. It is for people of India and history to judge whether these acts of bravery were patriotic or communal.

Were it not for political jealousy, its co-operation with the government of the day in rebuilding of this newly independent nation would have seen a wonderful utilisation of its constructive youthful energy. This was, perhaps, the idea in Sardar Patel's mind when he wrote to Guruji and told RSS to work with Congress Party. In his reply dated 11th September, 1948 to Shri Guruji, he had written, *"I have firm belief that Sangh people can do justice to their patriotism only by working together with the Congress and not by opposing it or being separate from it."*[1]

This well-referenced document is not for people who refuse to be convinced. A few Congress panelists and their supporters in debates claim that RSS never took part in 1963 Republic Day parade though there are newspaper reports and individual anecdotes of people who were present there. You can't open someone's eyes forcefully who don't wish to see. This book is for the people who really wish to know about RSS and its sustained work for the nation.

Communists and Left intellectuals have been at the forefront to give ideological cover to Congress offensive against RSS as beneficiaries of its largess in various forms. It would be educative to know what Communist party following international ideology of Communism was doing during these critical years. To put it pithily, Communist role in 1940s was highly dubious. Having given the call to armed revolution in 1940 against the British, the Communist Party of India (Note, it was not called Indian Communist Party) took a complete U-turn when Nazi Germany invaded the Soviet Union in June 1941 and Soviet Union and British ended up on the same side against Hitler. Consequently, the CPI offered to cooperate with the British in India. In return, in July 1942, the party was legalised by the government.[2]

The natural ideological progression made Communists support Muslim League's Lahore declaration of 22-24 March, 1940 for a separate Muslim nation. It declared that Muslim League was a secular party.[3] Communist Party of India passed a resolution in 1942 that India was a nation made up of multiple-nations and there were a minimum of 16 nations within it. They presented a proposal to Cabinet Mission in 1946 that India should be divided into 17 separate sovereign nations.[4]

When RSS and Akali Dal volunteers were busy saving Hindus and Sikhs valiantly and fighting the Muslim League promoted violence on the eve of independence, and trying to rehabilitate them, Communist took a totally different anti-national stance. They refused to accept this independence as true independence, claiming that it was anti-labour bourgeoisie government. This stand was in line with their overseas bosses' thinking. Joseph Stalin had declared on 9th February, 1951 that "we will not accept present situation in India (the first government led by Pandit Nehru) till socialist revolution succeeds there." Obeying this line, Communist Party of India had led an armed revolt in Telangana. E. M.S. Namboodiripad wrote in his biography, "Instead of learning its lessons from Telangana, it put in its efforts to repeat Telangana rebellion in entire nation. The policy was to establish its state power as per Telangana model and overthrow Nehru government.[5] Communist party finally called off its violent campaign on October 21, 1951, citing "increased repression by the Indian Army". It agreed to give up violent activities and function as a legal party using constitutional methods to acquire power.[6] We are aware that this blood-letting left its dormant seeds in Indian soil that sprouted first in the form of violent Naxalbari movement and much bigger and violent Maoist groups that are off-shoots of same Communist ideology. They are still the biggest threat to national integrity.

Discussions about historic changes in a nation's life need to take a holistic view and expand horizons while studying these changes. Unfortunately, monochromatic Left view or rather revision of current history of India has made it a sterile exercise as it tells us nothing about other streams of thoughts and people who fought for freedom of India.

Freedom was not achieved by 3-4 agitations or movements, a few individuals or one organisation. *Freedom rose slowly over a wave that had built up on the back of cultural renaissance triggered by great saints and spiritual leaders of Bharat.*

Dr. B.R. Ambedkar argues very well about rise of the political struggles over time. He says, "Political revolutions always take place after social and religious revolutions, this is proven principle of history. Normally, anyone will say so. Religious reforms movement started by Luther proved to be the forerunner of political liberty of European people. England's Puritanism showed the path to political freedom. Puritanism became the foundation of a new world. This Puritanism won the war of independence for America. And,

Puritanism was a religious movement. It is the same scenario in case of Muslim empire too. Arabians had to pass through the religious revolution set in by Hazrat Mohammad before Arabians could win political power. Even Indian history backs this theory. Buddha's religious and social revolution had preceded the political revolution under the leadership of Chandragupt. Political revolution of Shivaji took place consequent to the social and religious reforms brought in by saints of Maharashtra. Political revolution of Sikhs happened after Guru Nanak's religious and social revolution. It would be needless to give more examples. *For any nation to be liberated, it is a necessary condition that its heart and mind are liberated first*."[8]

Manmohan Vaidya, RSS joint General Secretary (Sahsarkaryavaah) takes the argument further. He writes, "Bharat is not just a political entity. *This is a cultural entity built over thousands of years of thought process based on perennial, comprehensive integrated life*. This philosophy of life gives us a unique identity woven together in a single thread of unity. Whenever there have been major political upheavals in India's history, they have been preceded by cultural awakening lit by spiritual energy. More difficult the situation, more awakened is the spiritual power of the nation. That is why, Bhakti movement rose through length and breadth of India during 12th Century to 15th Century. From Ramanujacharya in South to Swami Ramanand in North, every region saw a sustained tradition of Sadhus, Sants, Sanyasins and great spiritual leaders. During the British period, we saw the rise of Swami Dayanand Saraswati, Ramakrishna Paramhamsa and Swami Vivekananda that provided spiritual leadership. No political change has been successful or stable without such a cultural awakening preceding it. " He observes that we should realise, therefore, *that cultural awakening should not be measured on political parameters. Silent, sustained awakening is very important for a nation like Bharat.*[9] He underlines the fact that struggle for independence evolved and rose over decades of social reforms and raising the consciousness of the people by different leaders and organisations, including RSS.

It is time for Nehruvian eco-system to shut down its propaganda mills spinning flimsy yarns against RSS, an organisation that has inspired hundreds of thousands of Indians to dedicate their time and lives for selfless service to the society. I hope we in India will get over this partisan interpretation of historical and socio-political narrative; and get on with the most important job of renaissance of Bharat, that is, India.

India is free but she has not achieved unity, only a fissured and broken freedom. At one time, it almost seemed as if she might relapse into the chaos of separate States which preceded the British conquest. Fortunately, there has now developed a strong possibility that this disastrous relapse will be avoided. The wisely drastic policy of the Constituent Assembly makes it possible that the problem of the depressed classes will be solved without schism or fissure. But the old communal division into Hindu and Muslim seems to have hardened into the figure of a permanent political division of the country. It is to be hoped that the Congress and the nation will not accept the settled fact as forever settled or as anything more than a temporary expedient. For if it lasts, India may be seriously weakened, even crippled: civil strife may remain always possible, possible even a new invasion and foreign conquest. The partition of the country must go, – it is to be hoped by a slackening of tension, by a progressive understanding of the need of peace and concord, by the constant necessity of common and concerted action, even of an instrument of union for that purpose. In this way, unity may come about under whatever form – the exact form may have a pragmatic, but not a fundamental, importance. But by whatever means, the division must and will go. For without it, the destiny of India might be seriously impaired and even frustrated. But that must not be.

–Maharshi Aurobindo on 15th August, 1947

(Independence Day Message, Autobiographical Notes, CWSA, Vol. 36, pp 475-76)

References

Chapter-1

1. Dr. Hedgewar, N.H. Palkar, Marathi, 5th edition 2000, pages 21-22
2. ibid, page 37
3. Dr. Keshav Baliram Hedgewar, Rakesh Sinha, 1st edition, page 19
4. Blank
5. N.H. Palkar, op. cit., page 51
6. ibid, page 79
7. ibid, page 80
8. Dr. Manmohan Vaidya, Panchjanya, 11-12-2018, page 31

8A. ibid, page 83

9. ibid, page 88
10. ibid, page 91
11. ibid, page 98
12. Dr. Manmohan Vaidya, op. cit.
13. N.H. Palkar, op. cit., page 107
14. ibid, pages 109-110
15. ibid, page 105
16. Manmohan Vaidya, op. cit., page 29
17. Rakesh Sinha, op. cit., page 103
18. India Policy Foundation paper, http://www indiapolicyfoundation.org/slider1/Report%20 of%20the%20National%20Flag%20Committee.pdf; alsocrwflags.com
19. Rakesh Sinha, op. cit., ibid, page 104
20. ibid, 105

21. N.H. Palkar, op. cit., page 205
22. ibid, page 206
23. ibid, page 209
24. Rakesh Sinha, op. cit., ibid, page 111
25. ibid, page 110
26. N.H. Palkar, op. cit., Page 223
27. ibid, page 223
28. ibid, pages 286-287
29. Rakesh Sinha, op. cit., page 145
30. ibid, page 145
31. ibid, page 150
32. ibid, page 152
33. ibid, pages 153, 154
34. N.H. Palkar, op. cit., pages 265-267
35. ibid, page 300
36. F.M. Ghodke, Revolutionary Nationalism in Western India, pages 173-74, quoted in Rakesh Sinha, op. cit., page 182
37. Ratan Sharda, Prof. Rajendra Singh ki Jeevan Yatra, Hindi, 2014, page 29

Chapter-2

1. Ranga Hari, Guruji Golwalkar, Hindi edition, Year 2010, page 116
2. Ratan Sharda, op. cit., page 28
3. Manmohan Vaidya, op. cit., page 30
4. Ranga Hari, op. cit., page 116
5. Gobind Motwani, Jhamatmal Wadhwani, 9 years of RSS in Sindh – 1939-1947, Bharatiya Sindhu Sabha, 2006, page 58
6. Manmohan Vaidya, op. cit., page 30-31

6A. Sanjeev Kumar, Patna, email dated 10-12-2018

7. Ranga Hari, op. cit., page 116
8. ibid, page 117

8A. Dr. Mohan Bhagwat, recorded interview on 28-10-2018 in Keshav Srishti

9. ibid, page 117
10. ibid, page 117

11. Ratan Sharda, op. cit., page 28
12. ibid, page 26
13. The Hindu, dated 21-9-2004 https://www.thehindu.com/op/2004/09/21/stories/2004092100241400.htm
14. C.P. Bhishikar, Shri Guruji – Pioneer of a New Era, Page 97, translated from Hindi to English by Sudhakar Raje, 1999, Sahitya Sindhu Prakashana, Bengaluru
15. Ranga Hari, op. cit., page 111
16. Shridhar Damle email, quoting No.D. Home Pol. (Intelligence) Section F. No. 28 Pol.)
17. ibid, Home Department, Pol. F. No. 28/3/43-Pol (I)
18. Ranga Hari, op. cit., page 118
19. Devendra Swaroop, Sangh Beej se Vriksha, Hindi, Prabhat Prakashan, 2017 edition, page 64
20. ibid, page 64
20A. ibid, pages 60-61
21. India Today, 25-1-2016, Rahul Kanwal https://www.indiatoday.in/india/story/exclusive-attlee-told-bengal-governor-netaji-not-gandhi-got-india-freedom-claims-book-305512-2016-01-25 – quoting from Gen G.D. Bakshi's book on Netaji Subhas Chandra Bose – Bose – An Indian Samurai.
22. Three phases of India's struggle for Freedom, BVN Bombay, India, page 58-59, quoted in Manmohan Vaidya, op. cit., page 32)

Chapter-3

1. Ranga Hari, op. cit., page 122-123
2. ibid, page 123
3. ibid, page 123
4. ibid, page 124
5. ibid, page 124
6. ibid, page 124
7. ibid, page 125
7A. Manikchandra Vajpayee and Shridhar Paradkar, Jyoti Jala Nij Pran Ki, Hindi, Suruchi Prakashan, page 308-309

8. ibid, page 126
9. ibid, page 126
10. Manikchandra Vajpayee and Shridhar Paradkar, op. cit., pages 555-556
11. ibid, page 295
12. Ranga Hari, op. cit., page 127
12A. Karmayogini Mausiji, Hindi, Sevika Prakashan, Mathura, pages 51-52
13. Gobind Motwani, Jhamatmal Wadhwani, op. cit., page 129
14. Manikchandra Vajpayee and Shridhar Paradkar, op. cit., pages 245 to 247
15. Kuldip Chand Agnihotri, Jammu Kashmir ki Ankahi Kahani, Hindi, 35
16. ibid, page 238
17. ibid, pages 259-260
18. ibid, pages 260-262
19. ibid, pages 274-275
20. ibid, page 276
21. Ranga Hari, op. cit., pages 131-132
22. Narendra Sehgal, Vyathit Jammu Kashmir, Hindi, Year 2010, page 66-67
23. https://www.abplive.in/blog/key-sonia-gandhi-aide-in-his-memoirs-says-golwalkar-had-played-a-key-role-in-persuading-maharaja-hari-singh-of-jammu-and-kashmir-to-accede-to-india-712400
24. Ranga Hari, op. cit., page 132
25. ibid, page 133
26. Gobind Motwani, Jhamatmal Wadhwani, op. cit., page 108
27. ibid, page 125
28. Kuldeepchand Agnihotri, Jammu Kashmir ki Ankahi Kahani, Prabhat Prakashan, 2015, page 35
29. ibid, pages 472-487
30. ibid, pages 37-38
31. A.N. Bali, op. cit., page 18
32. Ranga Hari, op. cit., page 135

33. Now It Can Be Told, Prof. A.N. Bali, 1949, pages 137, 138
34. ibid, page 124
35. ibid, page 140
36. Ranga Hari, op. cit., pages 135-136
37. Manikchandra Vajpayee, Shridhar Paradkar, op. cit., page 17
38. ibid, page 17
39. ibid, page 314
40. ibid, page 59
41. ibid, pages 39-40
42. ibid, page 47
43. ibid, pages 49-50
44. ibid, chapter 4, pages 53 to 95
45. Ranga Hari, op. cit., page 139
46. ibid, page 139
47. ibid, page 144
48. Sampoorna Gandhi Vangmaya published by Publication division of Central
49. Ranga Hari, page 144
50. Ranga Hari, page 129
51. ibid, page 130
52. Independence Day Message, Autobiographical Notes, CWSA, Vol. 36, pages 475-76, quoted in Swarajya 16-3-16, https://swarajyamag.com/politics/sri-aurobindo-was-certainly-not-for-the-disintegration-of-india
53. Purushottam Shripad Lele, Dadra and Nagar Haveli: Past and Present, published by Usha P. Lele, 1987, Quoted in Wikipedia page on RSS – https://en.wikipedia.org/wiki/Goa_liberation_movement
54. H.V. Seshadri, RSS: Vision in Action, year 2000, page 28
55. Jaffrelot, Hindu Nationalist Movement 1996, p. 130, quoted on Wikipedia page on RSS - https://en.wikipedia.org/wiki/Rashtriya_Swayamsevak_Sangh
56. H.V. Seshadri, op. cit., page 28-29
57. Biography of Sudhir Phadke http://www.sudhirphadke.com/about/biography/

58. Mohan Ranade, Sarfaroshi ki Tamanna, Hindi, Vimal Prakashan, Pune, Second edition July 2015

Chapter-4

1. ibid, page 147
2. Ranga Hari, op. cit., pages 146-147
3. ibid, 147
4. ibid, page 147
5. ibid, 147
6. A.N. Bali, op. cit., page 138
7. ibid, page 139
8. ibid, 149
9. Ranga Hari, op. cit., pages 147-148
10. ibid, 149
11. ibid,149
12. ibid, pages 149-150
13. ibid, 150
14. ibid, page 153
15. ibid, page 153
16. ibid, page 154
17. ibid, page 155
18. ibid, page 157
19. ibid, page 159
20. ibid, page 157
21. ibid, page 160
22. ibid, page 168
23. ibid, page 168
24. A.N. Bali, op. cit., pages 141-142
25. Ranga Hari, op. cit., page 189
26. A.N. Bali, op. cit., page 144
27. ibid, pages 216-217
28. ibid, page 217

Conclusion

1. Ranga Hari, op. cit., page 169
2. Ishtiaq Ahmed, 25-9-2015, http://www.thefridaytimes.com/tft/how-far-left-of-partition/

3. Sandeep Dev, Kahani Communiston Ki, Hindi, 2017, page 151
4. ibid, pages 151-152
5. Sandeep Dev, op. cit., page 160
6. Amarnath K. Manon – 29-122-2007, https://www.indiatoday.in/magazine/cover-story/story/20071231-the-red-revolt-734843-2007-12-20
7. https://www.sikhnet.com/news/islamic-india-biggest-holocaust-world-history
8. Dr. B.R. Ambedkar – Jatipratha va tyanche nirmulan, Marathi, pages 15-16
9. Manmohan Vaidya, op. cit., page 32

**Biography of Shri Guruji by Ranga Hariji in Hindi, referred to in this book, is now available in English, titled "Incomparable Guruji", translated by Ratan Sharda and published by Prabhat Prakashan, New Delhi.*

❑❑❑